DISCOVER YOUR
OASIS

Escape Compassion Fatigue

By

William S. Cook, Jr., MD
Grant D. Fairley

Discover Your Oasis: Escape Compassion Fatigue
By William S. Cook, Jr., MD and Grant D. Fairley

Published By:
Silverwoods Publishing - a division of McK Consulting Inc.
Toronto ~ Chicago
www.silverwoods-publishing.com

ISBN 978-1-897202-32-6
Cover Design by Chickadee Photography
Cover Photo – EarthCaptured/bigstock.com

This book provides general information. Always consult your health professionals for advice on what is best for you.

Printed in the United States of America

First Edition

Dedication

This book is dedicated to all those in the caring professions, emergency services, educators, healthcare, public service, and those who care for loved ones. We salute your selfless acts of compassion and your commitment to the well-being of others. Your sacrifices deserve our honor and our deepest thanks.

Authors' Note

"And what about very old friends?" Gandalf asked at Bilbo's door.

Bill Cook and Grant Fairley met in 1977 at Wheaton College in Wheaton, Illinois, where Bill was a senior from the Deep South and Grant was a freshman from Canada. Like many schools, Wheaton paired older students with new ones to help them integrate into college life and hear the perspective of someone further down the road. These relationships were helpful for many incoming students, as was a great orientation program.

In the case of the two authors, it is a friendship that began there and has continued to this day. While we shared a liberal arts education at the storied school, our careers were destined to go in very different directions. Life eventually took Bill back to Mississippi, while Grant returned to Ontario.

It is a delight that our very different life journeys can now merge once again in the creation of this book, now more than forty years later.

Old friends indeed.

In addition to our own material, we are delighted to include chapters by four professionals. They generously shared their expertise and perspectives. This enriched our understanding about discerning, preventing, and recovering from compassion fatigue. This book is far better for the insights offered by these experts. It is our privilege to also call them our friends. Our sincere gratitude goes to Dr. Brenda Hines, Dr. Larry Komer, Dr. Blair Lamb, and Mr. Chris Redden for their contributions.

In Appreciation

Our editor did what all great editors do. Brittany Sanders Buczynski gave us a better book, while retaining our voices. Special thanks to Emma Fairley at Chickadee Photography for her assistance with our graphic design. Jeny Lyn Ruelo at Silverwoods Publishing - a division of McK Consulting Inc. was once again skillful and patient in assisting us.

Contents

Table of Contents

Introduction

We both were blessed to grow up in families where a commitment to serving others was a value that was modeled for us. We each had parents who cared for others professionally. Our parents were involved in serving others in their faith circles and in the wider community. Caring was given to us as an ideal to own and to practice.

Long before we met—with an international border and nine hundred miles separating us—we each saw great examples of caregivers in our extended families and close friends. It seemed quite normal to us that there were these noble, giving people everywhere in life.

As we grew older, we came to understand just how special these compassionate caregivers really were.

We have had opportunities in our careers to know the privilege of serving others. We both know what it is to burn out at times too.

In our journey, we are indebted to all the professors, professionals, colleagues, and writers that have prepared us for the roles we currently have. We have also learned so much from those we serve, as is usually the case.

These are our thoughts on what has helped us over the years as we have endeavored to serve others. Most of all, our reflections are intended to bring hope and encouragement to those who are caregivers.

Society includes many occupations that together allow us to care for the needs of today while creating a better tomorrow. Those in business champion the goods and services of our lives. Inventors and those in the technology field apply their knowledge and imagination to challenges and opportunities. Government supports individual, corporate, and international relationships through the laws and regulations necessary to create and maintain a civil society. Education creates common understanding while equipping individuals to explore life and work. Healthcare combats disease and explores wellness for this and future generations. Those who serve their faith communities connect the enchantment of faith with support for the needy here, while considering a life purpose and identity that transcends the temporal world. Artists call us to other places within and without ourselves.

We associate the idea of caregivers as those in the "helping professions," such as healthcare, social work, religion, and education. Yet, within most corporations, governments, organizations, and professions, you will find the caregivers. The human resources professional in a business, the customer service person at the counter, the tech support agent on the phone, the public servant in government who is trying to craft a solution to a seemingly intractable public policy challenge—these are just some examples of caregivers in less obvious places. Wherever you go, you will find people who are investing themselves into others.

Many become caregivers for a loved one who is afflicted with chronic illness, Alzheimer's, developmental needs, or other health challenges. This can be a spouse or partner, a parent, or a child who requires your time, energy, and commitment over an extended period of time.

Giving care has many rewards. The greatest of these is a deep satisfaction that comes when you know your efforts made a difference. Caregiving also can have a great price. The topic we will explore in this book is called compassion fatigue. Being compassionate, as you care for others, can drain you of your energy, your time, your health, and even worse, your hope. Many great people who have done great things for others end up burned out by the burdens they share with those they serve.

How do you continue to care without falling into the whirlpool of compassion fatigue? What choices can you make to have the emotional, physical, and spiritual stamina to keep on caring? Where do you find your oasis—that vital refreshment to invigorate and sustain your important work?

This book will offer hope to our weary caregivers who faithfully share their compassion and skills with those who need it most.

At the end of each chapter, you will see the initials of who wrote it. Here is a key to the initials.

WSC - William S. Cook, Jr., M.D.
GDF - Grant D. Fairley
BPH - Brenda P. Hines, M.D.
LDK - Lawrence D. Komer, MD, FRCSC
GBL - G. Blair Lamb, MD, FCFP
CLR - Chris L. Redden, LPC, NCC, CST

Discover Your Oasis

One night in 1885, war correspondent Charles Williams rode off alone into the desert. He had urgent news to share about one of the great military disasters of the Victorian era. Impatient with the slow progress of the returning military column, he had taken his camels and set out at night to reach the nearest town with a telegraph. He was a newsman, and this news needed to reach London, where the nation and the Empire anxiously awaited word of what had happened to Major-General Charles Gordon and the besieged city of Khartoum.

In the darkness, Williams missed the oasis, where food and water were stored to save the lives of those who journeyed in that unforgiving desert. Out of water, he was lost and alone for twenty hours. Each hour's heat and thirst weakened his body, until he was on the brink of severe dehydration. Death was now stalking him.

Finally, he came upon a village. He drank two gallons of water and a quart of milk. In his adventurous life, Williams had cheated death more than once. Now he notched another victory, as his strength slowly returned.

Williams was the first to report the news that Khartoum had fallen and Gordon was dead. The relief convoy had arrived two days too late to rescue Gordon and the city. Williams' later account in the *Fortnightly Review*, entitled "How We Lost Gordon," revealed the political and military misjudgments behind the tragedy. The scandal led to the resignation of many serving under William Gladstone in the British government.

Charles Williams was passionate to report the story. It was his work. It was his calling. Like the other war correspondents of his time, he was willing to take terrible risks and face great hardships in order to serve the public by telling the news.

Like Williams, the caring professions are filled with people who are passionate about their work of serving others.

They are the social workers who enter a troubled home. They are the nurses who stay late to help a patient in distress. They are the firefighters who race into danger. They are the ministers who feed the homeless. They are the teachers who inspire children to imagine. They are the physicians who answer the call to deliver a baby in the middle of the night. They are the sons and daughters caring for an aging parent. They are the government policy advisors who create solutions to complex challenges in society. They are the team at a hospice who provide end-of-life care and comfort to patients. They are the parents who sacrifice for their special needs child. They are the judges who hear cases that involve humanity at its worst. They are the nursing home professionals who care for failing bodies and confused minds.

Caregivers share who they are to make the lives of others better. They choose to serve rather than be served.

They are all around us in countless roles seen and unseen, caring for those in their charge. They keep the individuals, communities, and society itself from unraveling under the pressures that challenge body, soul, and spirit.

In a life that is committed to serving and giving, caregivers take many risks. First responders face physical risks. Many also risk their emotional health, as they see too many horrible moments in the lives of others. Some find their spirits crushed. Those who seek to inspire can themselves run out of inspiration. All live with the risk of burnout.

To serve others is to be willing to enter a desert to find those who are parched by the calamities, burdens, pains, disappointments, tragedies, and basic needs of life. Every hour that you are there begins to parch you, too. It is easy to forget to take care of yourself, as you concentrate on the needs of others. Passionate caregivers are at even greater risk because they are wired to think about others first. Little wonder that so many who care end up struggling with depression, addiction, discouragement, cynicism, bitterness, and other signs of burnout. The desert around us seems to encroach more and more into our professional lives.

How can caregivers avoid becoming a casualty?

Being in the desert can dehydrate you before you know it has happened. You must be purposeful in finding the refreshment you need.

If you must journey in the desert, visit the oasis.

Where is your oasis?

What can help you find the refreshment you need to carry on as an effective caregiver?

This book will help you discover your oasis.

While every oasis has the same basic necessities to allow you to survive, we believe that caregivers deserve better. We share ways to identify, create, and refresh your oasis so that you will not just survive— you will thrive.

Why is this important?

Your community owes you a debt that can never fully be repaid. You are someone who has chosen to be part of the solution. Yes, you will find satisfaction in your work. The pages of your life story will include the many moments you were there when others needed you. You may even hear a thank-you from those you help.

However, as long as you serve, and even long after you retire, burnout will hunt you. But there is always one place burnout can not find you: when you are at your oasis.

Society needs you at your best. As one of our contributors, Dr. Larry Komer, likes to say about his standard of care for his patients, "Only optimal is acceptable."

Optimal for a caregiver is the opportunity to bring your passion, commitment, personality, education, experience, spirit, curiosity, and energy to serve others. If you are burning out, those you serve will not experience you at your best.

No caregiver can function for long if they lose hope. Those who lose hope find despair. If your hope is waning, we are here to share hope with you. Even if you only see a small ember of hope still glowing, do not give up. Together, let's discover your oasis. It is your place of hope, especially for the weary caregiver.

GDF

The Passion in Compassion

What motivates people to go beyond doing their jobs just to earn a paycheck? How is it that some people truly excel in their work, surpassing the mere tasks necessary to complete the day's requirements? How is it that people who are careful, thorough, and do their work well, still may not be the very best in their field? What is the missing, magical ingredient?

In whatever their profession, trade, or task, people with passion bring a superior experience to all they serve.

What is passion?

Perhaps it is easier to understand if we take the question outside of the workplace. Think of activities, relationships, or interests where we might describe someone as being passionate. Sports, politics, religion, the arts, hobbies, and exploring nature are categories where we expect to see people showing passion. Being in love is one of the supreme examples.

Passion includes emotion, but it is more than just being emotional. It is an emotion that is directed or purposed. At its best, passion includes our whole being—spirit, soul, and body. The mind, the will, and the emotions are all engaged. Passion involves energy and heightened senses.

People who are passionate about their art often are "lost in the moment," transfixed by the experience of creating their painting, music, or story. Performers feel something extraordinary happening as they sing, act, dance, or play their music in front of an audience. They can feel that something greater than the sum of their knowledge and skills is at work when those talents are shared with passion.

At times, the emotional aspect of being highly passionate can create an imbalance that can cloud our thinking or lead to poor decisions. A "crime of passion" in the law recognizes this.

Passionate people can be enchanting or intimidating, depending on the focus of the passion and how they express it. It is especially interesting that extroverts, ambiverts, and introverts can all be passionate. While those passions may be expressed differently or in different contexts, the passion can be just as deep.

How does passion express itself in those who spend their careers in the helping professions? How can those who care for a parent with dementia or a child with special needs go beyond the necessary tasks that the care requires? How is it that they can have compassion? What is the passion in their compassion?

Compassionate people have developed the ability to go beyond an intellectual assessment of the needs of the people they serve. This is tied to the challenges faced by the patient, client, or loved one. No one feels compassion for someone who is well. It is only when there is suffering, challenges, or pain that compassion is engaged. Caregivers add an emotional dimension to the tasks they perform. Their work is not merely a series of functions to perform. They deeply care about those they are serving.

Why are some people more compassionate than others? It is a complex question, with many facets that could be explored. Consider these.

Compassionate people often have known their own suffering, disappointment, and pain. If you ask people who are in the helping professions, they often will have their own story to tell. They may have experienced an illness, a significant loss, or a battle with something in their lives. This has reminded them of how fragile we all are.

Many in the helping professions can point to someone who either helped them or inspired them. Being the recipient of someone else's care teaches us the difference a caring person can make. Observing a caring person can appeal to our ideals and challenge us to follow their example to make a difference.

A person's faith or ethical principles can also motivate him to serve others. When we believe that caring for others is a worthwhile use of our time on earth or that we have an ethical obligation to serve those in need, this can foster a very deep and abiding commitment to caregiving.

How a person experiences childhood can also be a significant factor. Those who have learned to be emotionally open and have experienced the practice of caring for someone understand what it feels like to show compassion to someone in need. The practice of kindness can lead to becoming a compassionate person.

This kind of compassion does not replace the value of training, competence, and excellence. But without compassion, acts of service remain just acts.

For all those who have allowed passion to flow into their compassion, we are grateful. Your whole-person engagement in the service of others is as transformative and enchanting as hearing a great song, gazing upon a great work of art, or watching an amazing performance.

Finding your oasis to avoid burnout will allow you to keep the compassion in your service and the passion in your compassion.

GDF

Hummingbirds and Camels

Hummingbirds are amazing creatures. They live life at speed, darting from bloom to bloom. Their wings beat so quickly that they can be mistaken for insects. As they drink the nectar from the blooms, they pollinate their flowers, which in turn will reproduce again and provide nourishment in the future.

For an animal who can keep on going over long distances with little refreshment, the camel comes to mind. Once watered, they can persist in their journey until they come to the next oasis.

Life in and of itself is a combination of marathons and sprints. As we get older, we understand the significance of the word *marathon*, but we also tend to understand there are periods of time in our lives that require bursts of energy, known as sprints. Everyone is familiar with the marathon, that grueling 26-mile race that challenges all parts of your body and mind. A sprint, on the other hand, is a brief explosion of energy in which we focus our efforts on a shorter goal, knowing that the sprint will be over in a short amount of time.

When we talk about caregiving, we know that it is for the long term. Many of us are called to be caregivers in our homes or in our professions. There is also a certain amount of caregiving that needs to occur within ourselves. When we look at a marathon, we are looking at the end of life, the challenge of continuing the race for the rest of our lives. We cannot make it through all of our lives without some sprints. If we did not take some time off and readjust our goals, our boundaries, or simply just rest, we would all suffer burnout at a much younger age than if we take care of ourselves in order to survive the marathon of life.

It is especially vital to take time out for ourselves when we are in the midst of caregiving for others. How do we manage the stress and sometimes the depression that builds up within us while we are caregiving? One of the most important things that we have talked about in other chapters is taking time for yourself; ensuring that you get enough rest, that you get enough exercise, and that you eat a healthy diet. We also must know what recharges our batteries. Identify those individuals or situations that give us strength, hope, and courage. During those times when we are not sure if we are going to make it through the marathon of life, it often helps to spend time with friends or participate in activities that give us solace and energy.

One of the ways to handle stress is to take a vacation. Vacations are essential to caregiving so that we do not become weary in the process. Some people take vacations overseas where there is no cell phone coverage in order to restore themselves. Others go to places in the mountains or perhaps to a sunny beach. Some of us like to take vacations away from caregiving by traveling alone, or with our spouse, or with our close family. Other times we might want to get away with a close friend that we trust and enjoy. Whatever type of vacation you prefer, carve out the necessary time away from your normal obligations. It is crucial to take breaks from life so that we can endure the marathon.

In addition to resting, taking breaks, or going on vacations, it is so important that we exercise. Exercise is essential for a healthy life. The type of exercise that we do depends on our stage in life, our schedules, and our finances. No matter what stage in life you are at, find an exercise you enjoy and schedule time to do it on a regular basis. Exercise actually energizes us, increases our vitality, and prolongs our lives.

If we are not engaging in regular exercise, we may feel sluggish, out of shape, or simply tired. In these cases, remember that it is much easier to exercise with a friend or a personal trainer as opposed to trying to do it by yourself. Start making small changes to improve your fitness. Perhaps it is just walking around the neighborhood a few times a week with a close friend. Or maybe you would like to try something more strenuous, like working out several times a week with a personal trainer doing CrossFit. There are all types of exercises. We must find what works for us and then incorporate that into our lives. We need to set time aside in our busy schedules to exercise, as without doing this, we will be more likely to develop the medical and/or emotional problems that go along with not exercising.

Exercising can create a close bond with others—perhaps your friend, your trainer, or those in the gym that you see on a regular basis. A sense of camaraderie can develop. When we are running the marathon of caregiving, these types of relationships in association with the exercise are essential.

The third key to managing stress and surviving a caregiving marathon is to eat a healthy diet. None of us live in an ideal world, and we are exposed to foods and snacks that are high in sugars, fats, and calories. Take time to look at your diet and what you are actually eating. Perhaps keep a food journal for a week to examine your eating habits. Many of us who are caregivers are rushed and do not take the time to eat well-balanced meals. We must recognize the importance of healthy eating as it ties into hope for being a weary caregiver.

Managing stress includes taking time to rest, taking time to exercise, and finally taking time to eat in healthy manner. These are ways in which we can survive the marathon of life.

All of us run into periods of time when we suddenly feel spent. Perhaps we have a sick parent or a sick spouse, or maybe if our profession is in the realm of caregiving, we might have some difficult patients or clients that are a challenge to our spirit, our will, or our emotions. When this happens, take a look at your life, examine your schedule, and try to plan times away from caregiving. This might include having someone cover for you on weekends if you are a physician or perhaps taking a few days off during the week if you are a minister. It might include a "mental health day" away from your job to do something relaxing and fun with somebody you care about so that your batteries can be recharged.

While we are in the midst of the marathon of life, sometimes we have to use extra energy, extra resources, and extra time. In other words, we have to sprint. These sprints are inevitable, but we must ensure that they are self-limited. We cannot sprint our entire lives. We will burn out. We will get physically ill or emotionally ill. We can sprint for short periods of time, in which we may not rest as much or eat as well or exercise as often. But knowing that the sprint is short-lived, we can make plans to recharge before we reenter the marathon of life.

So life itself is a marathon. We may be called to be caregivers in our jobs, in our homes, or with ourselves. It is important that we do not burn out or become weary in our caregiving. The way to do this is to set appropriate boundaries with your life. That includes your job, time with family, and time alone. We must also respect other individuals' boundaries so that they can achieve their goals in life.

Caregiving is an incredible opportunity and blessing in life. Helping someone else through a hard time, whether physically, financially, emotionally, or spiritually, can be quite rewarding. But we must not forget to take time for ourselves, maintain our boundaries, and remember the three different areas of taking care of ourselves in the process. This way, we will be able to manage the stress and hardships that will occur during the marathon of life.

WSC

Discover Your Sleep Oasis

Fatigue and excessive daytime sleepiness tend to occur in many caregivers as a result of inadequate and/or nonrestorative sleep. Many caregivers are chronically sleep-deprived, either due to the irregular sleep schedule of their affected loved one or due to the excessive demands of caring for their loved one, while attempting to meet their other obligations to work, family, etc. Caregivers may also be sleep-deprived because, with so much to do, they simply choose not to sleep as much as they actually could or need to sleep. Human beings cannot do without sleep, but the amount of sleep necessary to individual people varies widely, with six to ten hours being within the normal range. Average adult sleep time is seven and a half to eight hours.

Many caregivers suffer from insomnia with extended periods of nocturnal wakefulness and/or insufficient amounts of nocturnal sleep, despite adequate amount of time in bed. This is due to their stressful environment or circumstances. They may describe their sleep as poor quality or "non-restorative," even if the amount of usual sleep is perceived to be "normal" or adequate. Insomnia is a common problem and occurs when someone has trouble falling and staying asleep. Everyone has an occasional bad night's sleep, but insomnia means that you have trouble falling or staying asleep night after night. People with insomnia tend to be more irritable, depressed, and anxious. Getting your insomnia treated can help prevent you from developing depression. We know that people who have insomnia are ten times more likely to develop depression than people who sleep well. Many caregivers develop insomnia out of the necessity of remaining vigilant for their loved one during the night. This might include difficulty initiating and maintaining sleep, frequent awakenings, and early morning awakenings. Insufficient amounts of nocturnal sleep may lead to complaints of daytime fatigue, tiredness, or sleepiness, but also lack of concentration, irritability, anxiety, depression, forgetfulness, and impairment of motor skills or cognition, as well as psychosomatic symptoms such as aches and pains. Excessive daytime sleepiness, or hypersomnia, may be manifested by falling asleep in inappropriate places and circumstances.

Sleep deprivation may be acute or chronic. In either case, it poses a danger to the individuals experiencing it as well as to others, making one prone to accidents. The incidence of automobile crashes increases with driver fatigue and sleepiness. There is no easy test to determine if you are a danger to yourself or others due to exhaustion. People often can't judge how tired they are. Signs of drowsiness while driving include yawning, ending up too close to the next car, missing road signs or driving past turns, drifting out of the lane, and heavy eyelids. Not only does excessive daytime sleepiness adversely affect performance and productivity, it also affects quality of life and social interactions.

There is a strong relationship between sleep and mental health. When you have difficulty sleeping or experience poor quality sleep, your mental health often suffers. Also, a mental health condition may negatively affect your sleep. Both sleep disorders and mental health conditions impact your overall health and well-being.

Depression is one of the most common mental illnesses in the United States. People with depression often have trouble falling asleep or staying asleep. Some people sleep for more hours than usual when they are depressed. Signs of depression may include feeling sad most of the day (for days or weeks at a time), lacking interest in or not enjoying activities that usually make you happy, gaining or losing weight over a short period of time, feeling like you have no energy or are worn out.

Another common mental health problem involves anxiety. Everyone feels worried sometimes, but some people have anxiety disorders. People with an anxiety disorder may have trouble falling asleep at night or may wake up and be unable to fall back asleep. Signs of anxiety disorders may include worrying all the time (about large and small problems), breathing rapidly or having a racing heartbeat, feeling like you can't concentrate, sweating excessively, or having an upset stomach. It is interesting that mental health problems can be the cause of sleep problems, and sleep problems can be the cause of mental health problems.

Subjective sleepiness refers to the individual's perception of sleepiness. This can be dependent upon several external factors, such as a stimulating environment, ingestion of coffee or other caffeinated beverages, and prolonged periods of wakefulness. This increasing tendency to sleep after prolonged periods of wakefulness is called "sleep debt" and is aided by getting additional sleep. The recovery from sleep debt is not an exact number of hours of sleep, but the body needs an adequate amount of good quality sleep for restoration.

What happens when someone develops a sleep debt? What are the consequences of sleep deprivation? Sleep deprivation causes sleepiness, of course, but also poor performance, attention problems, poor concentration, difficulty completing tasks, and slower reaction time. Both total and partial sleep deprivation produce deleterious effects in humans. Psychometric tests have documented that sleepiness interferes with these higher cerebral functions and also can cause irritability, anxiety, and depression. In addition to these short-term consequences, chronic sleep deprivation causes a variety of long-term adverse consequences affecting several body systems and thus increasing the morbidity and mortality of the caregiver.

Shortened sleep duration is a risk factor for diabetes and obesity. Sleep deprivation may also contribute toward obesity by increasing hunger and appetite. After sleep restriction, hormone levels are disrupted, resulting in elevated evening cortisol levels, reduced glucose tolerance, decreased thyrotropin activity, increased sympathetic activation and altered growth hormone secretion, thereby increasing the risk for diabetes and obesity. Sleep deprivation also decreases production of leptin and increases production of ghrelin. Leptin is a hormone in adipocytes that stimulates the satiety center in the hypothalamus of the brain. This decrease in leptin increases hunger. Ghrelin is an appetite stimulant gastric peptide, which is increased with sleep deprivation. Thus an increase in ghrelin causes increased appetite and eventually increased BMI, which is also a risk factor for obesity and diabetes.

The chances of death from coronary artery disease, cancer, or stroke are greater for adults who sleep less than 4 hours when compared to those who sleep an average of seven and a half to eight hours per night. This suggests that there is increased mortality associated with sleep deprivation. Abnormal physiological changes after sleep restriction: reduced glucose tolerance, increased blood pressure, increased sympathetic activation, and increased inflammatory markers. One such inflammatory marker which is increased with sleep deprivation is C-reactive protein, an inflammatory myocardial risk. Sleep deprivation may result in insulin resistance, cardiovascular disease, and osteoporosis, due to decreased antibody production, decreased febrile response to endotoxin (fever), and increased inflammatory cytokines.

Sleep restriction and deprivation cause short-term effects, such as increased traffic accidents, excessive daytime sleepiness, and daytime cognitive dysfunction as revealed by psychometric testing, as well as long-term adverse effects, such as obesity, diabetes, osteoporosis, cardiovascular morbidity and mortality, and memory impairments.

What does all this mean to caregivers? Simply put, it is important to take care of yourself as well as your loved one. There are things that you can do to sleep better. You can improve common problem areas, create a good sleeping environment, and establish a healthy sleep routine. Eating too close to bedtime, heavy meals, or foods that upset your stomach can negatively affect your sleep. Regular exercise can help you fall asleep faster and sleep more soundly. Time your exercise to end over two hours before your bedtime to avoid trouble sleeping. Boredom and too little physical activity during the day can also make it harder to fall asleep. The artificial light generated by a laptop, tablet, or cell phone screen interferes with your body's sleepiness cues. To avoid this, turn off all electronic devices at least thirty minutes before bedtime. Make sure you have a comfortable bed in a dark, quiet room. Try blackout curtains or an eye mask if your room is too bright. Try a white noise machine or earplugs if your room is too noisy. In general, having a room temperature around 68 degrees is best for sleep. However, different people prefer hotter or colder rooms, so adjust the temperature if you are uncomfortable.

A healthy sleep routine includes getting up at the same time every day, even on the weekend or during vacations. Avoid taking naps if possible, or limit napping time to less than one hour. Never take a nap after 3:00 p.m. Only use your bed for sleeping, having sex, or recovering from illness. Have a regular schedule for meals, medications, chores, and other activities. This will help your inner body clock run smoothly. Find rituals that help you relax each night before bed. This can include things like a warm bath, a light snack, or a few minutes of reading. If you find yourself always worrying at bedtime, try to designate a specific time during the day to write down your worries and get these feelings out of your system. Try to have a regular sleep schedule, but don't go to bed until you are sleepy. If you are unable to fall or stay asleep within 20 minutes, get up. Try a quiet activity, and do not return to bed until you feel tired.

Check out common problem areas, such as caffeine. Caffeine stimulates the brain and interferes with sleep. Try to use caffeine as needed to help with tiredness in the morning. Regular use during the day can lead to sleep problems at night. Caffeine can impair sleep, and some individuals can be quite sensitive to just a tiny amount. If you are having trouble falling asleep, you should not drink more than 200 milligrams of caffeine a day, about the amount in two cups of coffee. Avoid any caffeine after lunch. Common sources of caffeine include coffee, tea, soft drinks, energy drinks, chocolate, and medications, including some pain relievers. Nicotine also stimulates the brain, causes you to have trouble falling asleep, and can make your sleep worse. Tobacco products like cigarettes and chewing tobacco contain large quantities of nicotine. If you quit smoking, your sleep may be worse while you are in withdrawal. After your body adjusts, you will fall asleep faster and wake up less during the night.

If you drink alcohol around bedtime, it may help you fall asleep since it slows brain activity. However, alcohol is bad for your sleep. It can make you wake up during the night and give you nightmares. You may also have a headache the next morning. Avoid alcohol within four to six hours of bedtime.

You may have to care for a loved one during your body's preferred sleep time and then sleep when your body wants to be awake. If you normally consider yourself a "night owl" and choose to go to bed late at night, you might have an easier time with the "night shift." Your body has an internal clock, which affects other body processes, like blood pressure and digestion. Your internal clock runs on approximately a 24-hour schedule that is called a circadian rhythm. Your body uses light to decide if it is night or day. Normally, you are alert during the daytime and sleepy at night. If there is a change in your environment, your body's circadian rhythm can shift over time. After shifting, you may be sleepy during the day and alert at night. When your time awake and alert does not match the time you need to perform your activities of caregiving, job, socialization, etc., you may have a circadian rhythm disorder. If you find it hard to fall asleep before 3 or 4 a.m. and then sleep into the late morning, you may have a delayed sleep phase disorder. If you find yourself ready for bed at 5 or 6 p.m. and then wake up as early as 2 or 3 a.m., you may have advanced sleep phase disorder. If you think you have a circadian rhythm disorder that is interfering with your ability to perform your necessary tasks, talk with your health care provider.

Circadian rhythm disorders may be treated with medications, melatonin, bright light therapy, or behavioral changes. Light exposure in the early-evening to bedtime period shifts the rhythm to a later time, decreasing the propensity to sleep (phase delay). Light exposure in the early morning causes a phase advance. The largest phase shifts are induced by very bright light, such as outdoor sunlight, but indoor light may also have an effect. Indoor sources of light have been used clinically to effectively shift the circadian clocks. Melatonin is a natural hormone produced in the brain that helps tell your body when it is time for sleep. Melatonin is secreted by the pineal gland only during darkness, and it appears to play a role in synchronizing the brain with the environment. Exogenous melatonin can produce phase-shifting effects, but the required timing of administration for a given direction of shift is opposite bright light and may require several days of melatonin doses before improvement is seen. It is available as an over-the-counter supplement.

All of this information is meant to convey one simple point: sleep is important. If you know the value of sleep, then you will likely make it more of a priority. Are you frequently tired, even after getting a normal amount of sleep? Try the sleep hygiene techniques mentioned earlier. If these do not work and excessive daytime sleepiness persists, seek professional help. Behavioral techniques for improving sleep are widely recommended as treatment for insomnia, but they are applied less commonly than the pharmacologic approach. Readily available educational materials and instruction by trained personnel may reduce clinician involvement and may make these techniques more cost-effective. Another option is cognitive behavioral therapy, which consists of eight to ten weekly sessions that provide education about sleep hygiene, stimulus control, and relaxation techniques. Cognitive behavioral therapy focuses on changing unrealistic beliefs and fears regarding the loss of sleep. There are even computer programs designed to assist the patient if cognitive behavioral therapy is too time intensive for the caregiver, or if the therapy is cost prohibitive. Two programs are available online, called "SHUTi" and "Night Owl Sleep Coach."

Relaxation therapy is another commonly used behavioral treatment. Many people with insomnia report physiologic (tension) and cognitive/emotional (racing thoughts and worrying) arousal at bedtime. Progressive muscle relaxation consists of first tensing then relaxing each muscle group in a systematic way. People with cognitive arousal at bedtime may benefit from meditation or guided-imagery techniques (focusing on a pleasant memory). Pharmacological treatments of insomnia are used by many health care providers temporarily or in some cases long term, depending on the circumstances. For some patients, knowing an effective hypnotic rescue is available decreases their anxiety about falling asleep. If sleep problems persist, please seek professional help.

How would one know when professional evaluation and treatment is needed? Subjective self-assessment of daytime sleepiness may help one differentiate between fatigue and a sleep disorder. The Epworth Sleepiness Scale measures average sleep propensity (chance of dozing) over eight common situations that almost everyone encounters. It is popular because it is a test that is simple and short. The propensity to fall asleep is rated as 0 (never), 1, 2, or 3 (high chance of dozing). The maximum score is 24, and normal is assumed to be 10 or less.

Take the test.

Here is a link from the Harvard Medical School that includes the Epworth Sleepiness Scale, as well as more information on sleep:

http://dev.healthysleep.med.harvard.edu/narcolepsy/diagnosing-narcolepsy/epworth-sleepiness-scale

Or use this Tiny URL to get to that page:

https://tinyurl.com/epworth-sleepiness-harvard

If the above score is 10 or higher, and previous efforts of improving sleep have been attempted (such as improvement in sleep hygiene, healthy routines, avoiding caffeine, etc.), one may benefit from discussing the problem with a health care provider. Some sleep disorders are very treatable, such as sleep apnea, narcolepsy, and restless leg syndrome. Sleepiness as a side effects of medications or other medical conditions should be ruled out before beginning treatment. Please discuss your symptoms with your health care provider or seek evaluation through a clinic that specializes in sleep disorders.

BPH

Called to Care

Those who are in the helping professions often have what they describe as a sense of "calling" into their caring role. The idea of being called includes some inspiration or pull that draws them to take on a difficult role that is, at its heart, others centered.

They may be following the example of a parent, family member, or family friend—someone who was instrumental in their choice to join in the same serving profession or some other caring community. This could include the familiarity of the occupation, as is true of many others who follow in a parent's footsteps. However, those in the helping professions will often speak of a deep sense of satisfaction that they witnessed in the parent or other person who was a caregiver. Sometimes, this is in spite of the cost and commitment required to be there in the service of others in need.

If not inspired by someone close to them, caregivers may also be influenced by some type of mentor in their lives who guided and encouraged them to consider a certain field for their career. Those who have developed a spiritual dimension in their lives may express that they were led by God to go on this or that path of service. Some others have an inner sense of some type of calling to help others, based on experiences that they had when they were children. It is very common for mental healthcare workers in the substance abuse field to have struggled with their own addictions when they were younger. Having survived their struggle, they want to help those who have similar difficulties.

Some people have a natural aptitude for caregiving: a heightened awareness of the needs of others and the ability to care for them well. They may find that they seem innately gifted to work with others who are in a challenging time. Their experiences light the way for their educational and career choices, just as engineers, architects, and entrepreneurs have a predisposition to their endeavors.

We believe that any career can be a force for good, even if you are not in the classic roles of caregivers. Not all can or should be nurses, social workers, teachers, or others working in the compassionate fields. Many people who are not employed in a helping profession volunteer their free time to compassionately care for others in the community. The special needs or chronic illness of a family member, spouse, or friend may occupy a person's life outside of the workplace. These acts of selflessness are no less noble or important than full-time caregiving. To those who receive their compassion, it is life-changing.

Those in the helping professions who see their work as more than an occupation, who add compassion to their skill set, will often tell you that they answered some sense of a call that seemed to draw them relentlessly into this area of service. Our communities are better because they answered "yes" to the need that was before them.

GDF

Mindfulness: Your Mental Oasis

You may have heard about the term "mindfulness." While it is a relatively new term, it is not a new concept. The concept of living in the present, meditation, and paying attention to what is around you goes back to biblical times and may be found in many other ancient traditions as well.

Mindfulness is an important antidote to an ever-changing and highly demanding world. Pressures of past, present, and future can crowd out the opportunities to "take time to smell the roses," as it was poetically put. It is important for all of us to be intentional to make time to live in the moment. Many of the worries that consume us are about future events that may or may not happen. Many also live with feelings of regret and guilt about past choices.

By taking time to reflect on the present, allowing your mind and emotions to quiet, you begin to gain some perspective. It does not change the past or solve the future, but it equips you to be stronger as you go through your day.

Some people practice mindfulness by spending time in nature, and in doing so, they allow something else to be their focus. Embracing the sights, sounds, smells, and feelings of being in the woods or visiting a garden can refresh your thoughts.

People of faith often use times of prayer and meditation to regain perspective. The opportunity to sit silently or to contemplate can serve to remind you of your place in the greater story.

Quiet music can also aid your time of mindfulness. The gentle sounds can help dampen the noise of thoughts and worries that may be distracting you from clearing your heart and mind.

There is no right or wrong way to practice mindfulness. There are many helpful books on different techniques. Most people find their own way, since mindfulness usually reflects a person's preferences. Looks for ideas that help you relax and find your inner quiet.

Mindfulness involves letting go of control and releasing fear and worry. Like anything important in life, it is a matter of practice. It can seem strange at first. We are not familiar with quiet anymore. As you experience it again and again, it will become more comfortable each time. After a while, you will notice when you have missed it. Before long, you will look forward to that time of reflection.

The serenity prayer in the Alcoholics Anonymous recovery program gives attention to mindfulness when it asks for wisdom to know the difference between what we can and cannot change. We must change what we can, not live in fear, and accept what we are unable to change.

Practicing mindfulness, even just ten minutes a day, can improve depression, lower anxiety and worry, and increase happiness. If we remain focused on the moment rather than fearing the future or worrying about our past, our bodies respond physically by lowering blood pressure or calming gastrointestinal problems. If you suffer from headaches, research has shown that mindfulness can make headaches shorter and less severe. Our bodies respond to mindfulness by being happier, less depressed, and less anxious.

Some individuals who have a harder time practicing mindfulness than others. This includes those that are suffering from clinical depression, anxiety, or obsessive-compulsive disorder. If you need to seek professional counseling for dealing with mindfulness, do so.

Mindfulness is not denial. Issues from our past should be addressed. Solving problems in our present is necessary. Planning well for the future is wise. Being someone who practices mindfulness allows you to be better equipped to fully live your life.

WSC

Three Short - Three Long - Three Short

Long before LOL, IDK, and TTFN was the universal distress signal SOS. In the age of telegraphs and later radio, everyone knew this Morse Code message: ...---... (three short, three long, three short). It meant SOS—Save Our Souls. This was the distress message for when disaster had struck and lives were at risk. These sounds conveyed the urgency of needing someone else's assistance immediately. By definition, this was not something you could handle on your own.

I always thought that it was interesting that the phrase was "Save Our Souls," not "Save Our Bodies." It was a very human appeal. We are more than just flesh and blood.

Those who are caregivers are the ones who will hear someone sending them a distress signal. Sometimes, it is not audible, but it is very clear. The calling to care is triggered, and the amazing work of the caregiver engages that soul in need.

For the caregiver, it is much more difficult to issue an SOS message. The stresses of being there for those in crisis and for those with a chronic need take their toll on even the most well-trained, positive, and resilient caregivers. Those in the helping professions have their focus on the well-being of others. It is not natural for a caregiver to consider the challenges that are stressing them. They are often great at taking care of others. Taking care of themselves? Not so much.

Even if a caregiver recognizes that they are stressed out or at risk, they are reluctant to be off the front lines where they are helping others. They are certainly not in favor of the scarce resources in the system being used for their support, when so many others with far greater challenges need the attention. The very noble qualities of self-sacrifice, which make these professionals so valuable in supporting and caring for others, prevent them from asking for help.

As you speak with people who feel called to care for others, you often find that they have experienced some pain, hurt, or tragedy in their earlier life. These disappointments and challenges create sensitivity toward the needs of others around them. They know what it is like to suffer. Their painful experiences are channeled into a better purpose. Caring for others allows them to make some sense out of all of the anguish they have experienced along the way.

Sometimes it is the example of a caregiver who helped them through their dark times that motivates them to care for others. Many caregivers also have older members of their family who were in the helping profession. While observing the stresses and hours required to be in a caregiving role, younger family members also recognized the sense of satisfaction that their elders derived from a life serving others. It is not an easy life, but it is a life worth living.

For those who are mentors and forerunners of the next generation, it is important to share not only the joys and the value of being a caregiver but also the stresses and strains. Learning that these giants in your life also struggled in their roles can be powerfully reassuring. It helps the caregivers to have realistic expectations about the profession. You do not need to be a superhero to make a difference.

When the pressures start to build, that is time to seek support. We tend to procrastinate because we are too busy to veer off the demands of our schedule. There is always one more appointment to keep, one more client to meet, one more crisis that needs you to be present.

Stresses caused by living from crisis to crisis accumulate. The grinding work of chronic care has a more subtle stress, but it builds too. Like an unpaid credit card, the balance keeps growing because the high rate of interest is added. The bill for being in a stressful occupation must be paid sooner or later. It is always less expensive to pay it sooner.

What does that mean for the caregiver? How can you manage the stresses that are part of the job?

As discussed in this book, discovering your oasis will give you a place to recover and refresh. The oasis experience allows you to releases stress, regain perspective, and renew your satisfaction. Regular self-care enhances your ability to care for others more effectively.

What do you do when an event or an accumulation of stresses has you at the breaking point? Tensions are high. Those in your life sound warnings that you and your relationships are not doing well. Sleep becomes elusive. Concentration is difficult. Anxiety and depression cloud your days. "Houston, we have a problem."

We practice fire drills so that we know what to do when a fire breaks out. Where are the exits? What do we do? What do we *not* do? Where do we meet? The practice allows us to override our stress of the moment and get to safety because we know what to do.

If a crisis breaks out in your professional or personal life, what is the drill? Who would you call? What would you do? What steps would you take to be safe? Those who have thought this through and have a plan have made an important career decision. It also is a statement to your family and friends that you value them, too.

Make a list of specific things you would do in a personal crisis. Test your list by discussing it with a colleague. Include your significant other or family members in the discussion so that they can also be eyes and ears to alert you to a stress spike. Give them permission to ask how things are going. Invite them to speak up when they are concerned.

Thankfully, many organizations recognize this fact and create regular check-ups for those who spend their careers supporting others. This is so important to have a sustainable model for serving the patients, clients, congregations, or the public.

If you have a career that includes caring for others, it is a question of "when" not "if" you will face your own crisis. When that happens, declare your emergency. Start tapping ...---... SOS. Say Mayday. Yours is a soul worth saving. Let others help the helper—even if it is you.

GDF

Surviving Your 20 Percent

Odzala is a national park founded in 1935 in the northern part of the Republic of the Congo. Odzala is a magical place filled with exceptional beauty and solitude and incredible nature. Located in a very remote area of the world's second largest rainforest, Odzala is an oasis in the midst of Africa. It is a place where you can go and restore your batteries and take in a wide variety of encouraging experiences.

It has been said that 80 percent of our problems come from 20 percent of the people. You will find that this is the case if you work in any type of business that deals with the public. It can also occur in any type of group setting, such as business committee meetings or even committees for charity functions. How do we cope with those chronic complainers, the 20 percent that try to drain us of our emotional, spiritual, and physical energies?

You can survive by setting boundaries with these individuals, while also finding your oasis in life and going to that oasis to restore yourself. There are many types of oases that we can go to for refreshment and rebirth. Not all of us can travel 10,000 miles to Odzala National Park in the Republic of Congo to restore our batteries. What we can do is identify what gives us refreshment and rest and nourishment for ourselves, and then make time to do those things, so that we can continue on with life dealing with those 20 percent. It would be a misconception to think that the 20 percent are just going to go away, that we will not have to deal with them or can somehow avoid them. Knowing that this is the case, it is important to find out how to cope with chronic complainers.

Identify the oasis in your life. Your oasis might be anything from taking a day trip alone to the beach or even just reading a book that you enjoy in your home when no one is around. Your oasis might be overseas travel, or it might be travel in short distances. Some people find refreshment in getting a relaxing massage or going to a yoga class. Some find refreshment in their souls by just being alone. There are others with extroverted personalities that are stimulated and refreshed by going to a party. Some of us like to be around lots of people and require social interaction to restore our batteries. Some of us need peace and quiet to feel rested and refreshed. The main thing is to identify which type of person you are, understand what you need in order to be recharged, and then go to your oasis in life. Going to your oasis is not a one-time experience. It may be going overseas for one oasis experience, but spending time with a close friend for another oasis experience.

These oasis experiences do not have to be the same, but they could be. Your oasis experiences need to be easily accessible to you. Some people have found that the best way to cope with the 20 percent of chronic complainers in their lives is to set aside some time each day for meditation, for reflection, for quietness. Many find their oasis in God and discover that they are able to be refreshed and nourished through their relationship with him.

The other part of coping with chronic complainers (and we all know who those people are) is to set boundaries. The setting of boundaries, which was discussed in another chapter, is essential to healthy living.

Sometimes those chronic complainers can complain and complain and complain, slowly draining us of the joy that we need for life. There are those chronic complainers who want to change their lives and be more positive people; however, there are a lot of chronic complainers who just like to complain and have no desire to change. Many times they do not even know they are chronically complaining. It is just a natural habit. When dealing with these people, ask open-ended questions to find out what the complaint is and why they are complaining. But when you have done all that you can do to help them, it is time to set a personal boundary, so that they do not continue to rob you of your joy and energy.

Setting boundaries might include limiting phone calls or personal interaction with complainers. It might even involve not picking up the phone when a certain name or number turns up on caller ID. It might involve un-friending someone on Facebook. It might involve referring a business customer or a patient to someone else. There is a certain point in time when the 20 percent complainers cause the recipient of these complaints to build up resentment. Once resentment starts building up, the line has been crossed, and something must be done to correct it.

Occasionally, we must directly confront the complainers and let them know that we have done all that we can do, perhaps even being frank enough to tell them they should quit complaining. Sometimes it is important to point out complainers and the complaints, and if there is really nothing to complain about, it is okay to ask for an apology. It is unlikely that you will get an apology, but it never hurts to ask.

Boundaries come in all forms, shapes, and sizes. Boundaries can be limits that keep us emotionally healthy. They can be limits with our jobs, our friendships, our families, and the chronic complainers in our lives. It is impossible to avoid complainers. They are out there in wide numbers. What we can do is limit the amount of complaints that come into our world and try to rob us of joy. Never lose sight of what your oasis is and go to it as much as you need to, so that you can live a happy, joyous life.

In summary, 20 percent of the people are known to cause 80 percent of the misery. Enjoy the 80 percent of people who are pleasant and set boundaries with the 20 percent who are not. Limit the negative effects on your life from the 20 percent of complainers. Try to address their problems as best you can, and when you have addressed those problems to the best of your ability, set a boundary. It is really best for you and the other person to have clear boundaries about what you are willing and able to tolerate and what you are not. Go to your oasis frequently. Identify what that is and lead a joyous, happy life full of energy, compassion, and mindfulness.

WSC

All's Well:
Your Emotional Oasis

My great-grandmother, Jean Cowan, had a very old, colorful figure on her mantle. It was a tall man, with a drawn face. His hat and a flowing blue robe spoke of medieval times in Britain. In one hand was a lit lamp. In the other was a tall halberd, a weapon with reach, a pointed end and an axe included too. He was a night watchman.

The task of the night watchman was to patrol his wall or area of the town at night. This was a part of life during a time when towns were never very secure from bandits, marauders, or a nearby cranky clan. On the hour, each of the watchmen would call out the time and then say, "All's well!" If there were other watchmen, they too would call out in response. When people heard these words, they were able to relax in their homes and later sleep soundly. All was well.

Having raised nine children of her own, been a grandmother to many more, and now as a great-grandmother, Granny Cowan was someone who knew how to keep children engaged. She would sing us songs, show us interesting objects, and tell us stories. This figure, safely out of reach of inquisitive children, would be one of the regular topics to discuss. "Nine o'clock, and all's well!" "Ten o'clock, and all's well!" We would always include some version of that on our visits to her old home on Oakwood in Toronto. He became known not as the night watchman, but as "Allswell."

The life of a caregiver takes that person into the lives of others where all is not well. Often, very little is going well. The role of those in the helping professions includes supporting, sustaining, and sometimes sheltering those who are vulnerable, so that one day they may be able to return to a place where all's well. Using your education, training, skills, and compassion, you will be one of those sources of hope, insight, and comfort for someone in need. The energy required as a caregiver can be physically draining. It will often be emotionally draining too.

How can you discover your emotional oasis?

Our emotional life is very complex. It is impacted by our relationships, health, history, and work. For most people, it is still a largely foreign, unexplored country. The emotional landscape in which we live is constantly changing with the forces of life and time.

We touch on a number of aspects of our emotional world elsewhere in this book. Depending on your profession, your work may be largely focused on the emotional challenges facing your patients or clients. If so, you already understand the intensity of the world of emotions.

Where is your emotional oasis? It is the place where you, too, can say, "All's well!"

GDF

Drawing the Lines

When we think of the word *boundaries*, we may think of physical boundaries like the Great Wall of China, or a moat around a castle, or perhaps even a security fence around our property. Boundaries are considered limitations in some ways, but they offer us the opportunity for a very abundant, happy, healthy life. Without appropriate boundaries, our lives would be chaotic and in total disarray. When we look at boundaries in the context of this book, we think of those boundaries that help us be the caregivers that we need to be but also protect us from getting burned out, depressed, and anxious.

Yes, boundaries can be a physical structure, but this chapter focuses more on the boundaries that we cannot see yet must have in place in order to not become worried caregivers. Let's consider some examples of boundaries that are not per se physical in nature but are helpful, such as schedules or rules for our use of time. We could consider a boundary as the time we go to work.

When we start our job in the morning (or evening), we have a boundary between our personal life and our work life. When the clock goes off at perhaps 8 or 9 a.m., our personal life is put on hold for the next eight to ten to twelve hours. We switch gears in our minds and focus on a different set of issues and problems than what we might face at home.

Some people are caregivers in their jobs during the day and then also have to take on a caregiving role in the evening when they return home from work. Some people perhaps do not have the luxury of going to work; they have to provide full-time care for a family member who is ill or disabled. You do not have to be a minister or a physician to be a caregiver. If you look at caregiving in the broadest sense of the word, we are all caregivers in whatever role we find ourselves in at the time. Maybe you are a parent and are taking care of your children. Maybe you are a schoolteacher and are taking care of your students. Maybe you deliver the mail and take care of your postal clients. There are so many different ways that caregiving presents itself in our lives.

When we look at caregiving, we need to look at both the caregiving of ourselves and the caregiving of others in our lives. Caregiving of others might include those in our jobs (clients, patients, customers) or in our personal lives (children, aging parents, a friend in need). That is the most important boundary that we will address in this chapter. The boundary is this: where do we begin and end, and where does someone else begin and end. We must decide this for ourselves on a daily basis. This boundary may be fluid. As we become older, it is often very clear to us that boundaries we thought were black and white when we were younger have become more blurred with shades of gray. The most important boundary, though, is the boundary for self-protection and self-preservation. If we do not maintain appropriate boundaries with others, we will be ineffective caregivers and ineffective in other parts of our lives.

Boundaries are the framework of society. In addition to a physical boundary such as a fence, you might think of the imaginary boundary that delineates the state, province, or country in which you live. We all have boundaries or borders that delineate this as our country and that as another country. Those boundaries are much clearer than the emotional boundaries that we are forced to deal with on a daily basis. We may have reached the point in our lives where we perceive that we have nothing to offer other people. We may feel we are unable to give to other people because we are so worn out ourselves. In these cases, we might be the recipient of care, whether emotional, physical, or financial. No matter what stage we are at in our lives, there is always the potential for being the caregiver to others as well as receiving care.

Healthy boundaries help contribute to good mental health. For example, in our technology-saturated world of text messages, e-mails, the Internet, and telephones, we have the option of creating our own boundaries. We can make the choice of not answering a text or an e-mail or a telephone call at a certain point in time. That is the boundary that we must use at times to preserve and protect ourselves. Instant accessibility, which has become the hallmark of our modern-day society, has led to weariness among caregivers.

It is possible, without boundaries, that the caregiver might feel that they are on-call all the time (24/7) and that they never get a break. Even in many of the remote areas of Africa and Asia, there is Internet, there are e-mails, and there is the ability to send and receive text messages. You can travel thousands of miles from where you live, but if you do not maintain boundaries on accessibility, you will get fatigued and weary and possibly quite depressed and anxious. So, what do we do to establish or maintain boundaries in our lives? It comes down to setting time limits and schedules regarding who we interact with and who we give our time to.

No matter what we do in life, no matter how prestigious our job or how mundane, we all have twenty-four hours in a day to do what we can do to help others and ourselves. We must get adequate sleep in order to feel well rested to do our duties during the day. Everyone needs rest. Everyone needs an appropriate amount of sleep to be a caregiver.

With that being said, that leaves us perhaps fourteen to sixteen hours of our waking day to help ourselves or other people. One way that we help ourselves and establish boundaries is through employment. We all have bills to pay, and most of us have to work or choose to work to financially provide for our families.

For many of our jobs, one boundary is that on Friday afternoon at 5 o'clock, work for the week is over. That is what a weekend is; it is actually a boundary from work before restarting Monday morning with our jobs. When we think of caregiving, we typically think of perhaps caring for an elderly friend or a parent in a home setting. But no matter where we are or what we do, we are all potential caregivers. Even in our jobs, caring for others, we may overdo it and experience burnout. No one can work day in and day out without a break and without time off. I am a big believer in vacations, taking extended time off from work, as a boundary to recharge batteries and restore our mental and physical health. Taking time out from our caregiving roles is essential to maintaining the ability to care for others.

When it comes to caring for a sick individual, we need to establish a network of caring individuals. One person cannot do it alone. The caring team might include a hospice nurse or a home health nurse or a nurse's aide. It might include a neighbor, a friend from church, or a family member. It has been said that it takes a village to raise a child. It also takes a village to care for chronically ill individuals. As much as you care for that individual, you cannot do it alone. You must have help. You must ask for help. We all must allow others to assume caregiving roles in our lives.

One of the biggest blessings for a caregiver is when the recipient receives that care with thanks and appreciation. That can do more than you can imagine for the caregiver's self-esteem and sense of fulfillment. Just feeling appreciated and cared for themselves is so important. Caregiving is actually a two-way street in many ways. We stereotypically see it as a one-way street in which the caregiver gives some type of care to the sick or disabled individual. But what the caregiver receives by giving to another person is quite a blessing in itself.

In summary, boundaries are essential in our lives. Setting proper emotional boundaries and time boundaries is essential for good mental health and our ability to help other people. Strong boundaries allow you to maintain a healthy life yourself and be the best you can be. Without boundaries, there is chaos in our lives and in the world. At times, boundaries must be moved in one direction or the other, but they must always be protected. It is important to know what your boundaries are and what you need, so that you do not get burned out and become depressed or anxious. A wise caregiver sets wise boundaries.

WSC

Old Friends: Your Social Oasis

One of the greatest titles we can have is "Old Friend." However, we never truly appreciate how important old friends are until we grow older.

The problem is that we need to start our old friendships when we are young. We then have to nurture and grow those friendships over our middle-age years, when a busy life and changing geographies can cause us to neglect those friends.

Those in the helping professions especially need to have old friends.

With the challenges of serving others, you often find that you cannot socialize in the same way that you could before. How many times have you had people approach you in a social situation to ask your professional advice? Have you ever wanted to reply, "Who are you talking to right now—me the person or the professional on my business card? Would you be as interested in me if I did something else for a living?"

Old friends are different. Those relationships stretch back before we had success or money. These friendships are the ones that we knew were authentic, since there were no other motivations to cloud the relationship.

A feature of old friends is that they understand more of your history.

They have been in your story for a long time and may have walked with you through the mountaintop experiences as well as the dark valleys that are included in your tale. Hopefully, you have been there for them through their ups and downs too. The fact that they still accept you is so affirming.

Taking time to cultivate relationships outside of the workplace is vital. If work is all-consuming to the point that we do not have time for friendships, it is likely that we are undermining our capacity to care over the long term. Without the refreshment and interaction that genuine friendships provide, people tend to lose some of the authenticity that healthy relationships bring.

This is especially true if you are in a position where people tend to be deferential to you. It is easy to begin to see your relationships from a layered perspective. You perhaps have seen the great cartoon where the boss is introducing an employee to someone by saying, "May I introduce you to my immediate inferior, Bill Smith?" It is easy in those environments to confuse someone's respect and deference to your position with you being a superior person.

Friendships, by their very nature, are about equality. You may have varying degrees of intimacy, from an acquaintance to a close friend to a best friend, but they are all based on being friends.

Friends are not superior or inferior.

Spending time with friends, and especially old friends, brings us back to the reality that we are who we once were. We have added new life experiences and perspectives to our stories. That only makes our friendship more interesting. There is an unconditional foundation in our great friendships. Not to be confused with approval, it does mean that we cut each other a great deal of slack.

Some people will tell you it is okay to be brutally honest with your closest friends. I do not believe that this is true. Instead, the more important your friendship, the more care you must take to protect it and treat it with respect. The safe places that our best friendships afford can be damaged by careless words or taking them for granted. Treat your greatest friendships with the respect you would afford anything of great value in your life. Be authentic, but be careful. Friendships—even grand, old friendships—can break, if we do not pay attention.

Keeping old friends does take work, often during the busiest times of life, when careers and other obligations are at their peak. Caregivers especially need to make time to be with their friends. The temptation is to assume that you can wait until things are not so busy. Then you will catch up. Perhaps those friends will be there for you then. Maybe they will be gone. What you will have lost (and they will have lost as well) is the benefits of friendship during times of your life when it might be the most helpful. Friendship is a great antidote to the arrogance of power because friends will not tolerate it.

If you have not continued to be in touch with your friends, restarting those relationships may be awkward at first. It may be uncomfortable for someone from the old neighborhood to connect with you in a different stratum of economic life. You do need to be sensitive to that in making your connections. Some people will be reluctant to connect again for fear that they could not afford the restaurants where you might go, for example.

Visiting your home might make them self-conscious, if they feel that you would be uncomfortable in their home.

Some people handle another's generosity comfortably on the basis that if the roles were reversed, they too would do the same. Others find it difficult because they feel that they have not achieved what you have.

In all friendships, these are things you have to sense with each other and find what is comfortable and what works. That will take some care and sensitivity, as well as a commitment to keeping the friendship alive and well.

So if you have not been in touch with some old or current friends for awhile, why not pick up the phone, send an e-mail, or open WhatsApp or Skype? Keep those connections alive and well.

Perhaps the greatest rewards in friendship come in the later years of life. When the intensity of serving others mellows with age, your life passages concentrate more and more on relationships. You are more aware of the importance of your children, grandchildren, and siblings.

You begin to realize in a deeper way that it is not what we do or what we have that makes us who we are. Old friends are people who recognize that and understand us best at that stage of life.

Right now you are probably making investments in your retirement saving accounts, planning for a golden retirement. Be sure to make investments each and every year in your friendship accounts as well. That may be the most valuable part of your portfolio when you are retired.

Who would you like to have as an old friend when you reach the final stage of life?

Today is the day to invest in those people we hope will call us "old friend" in the years to come.

GDF

Refilling Your Reservoir

When your compassion reserves are running low or even on empty, how can you build them up? What can you do to refill your reservoir of emotions and energy? This is a very important question when you are in the role of caregiving. It is essential to know how to refill your reservoir so that you can continue to be a compassionate caregiver to others.

One of the obvious things that we can do to build up our compassion reserves is to take time to rest. This may be taking an afternoon off from work. It might be going to a movie. It might be spending the day with a close friend. It might be going on a personal retreat. To take these steps, you must first be aware of when your emotional reservoir is draining out and running on empty. You must be able to identify when you need to take those steps to build up your compassion reserves.

I find that, personally, my reservoir is refilled with overseas vacations. When I go to places such as South Africa, there is limited cell phone service and text messaging. Instant availability is no longer possible. Unplugging myself from social media, the Internet, and 24-hour news channels helps me refill my reservoir. Going on photographic safaris and taking in the beauties of nature help me build up my compassion reserves. It is during these times that I focus on taking care of myself and letting others take care of me and encourage me and show compassion to me. Of course, you don't have to travel overseas to experience these benefits. Simply turn off your cell phone for the weekend. Go camping or hiking and take in the beauty of nature. Find something that recharges your batteries.

I also find that my reservoir is refilled by sharing burdens with close friends. By talking to a close friend or just spending time together, I can rebuild my compassion reserves. One of the ways that I refill my reservoir is to do Cross Fit exercises. These routines allow me to challenge myself and get the satisfaction of completing tasks that are physically strenuous. I also get the positive feedback from my trainer, telling me that I have done a good job or that I am doing the exercise right. I find that when someone shows me compassion, I am better able to be more compassionate toward others.

Of course, we cannot make somebody be compassionate toward us, but we can focus on ourselves and try to be compassionate towards others. When we offer others encouragement and support, many times those around us become more likely to show compassion to us.

Sometimes we have burdens that we are scared to share with family, friends, the clergy, or a mental health professional. Sometimes we unnecessarily drain our reserves by not letting someone else share in our burdens. When I share my burdens with a friend or clergy or another type of professional, my reservoir is refilled and my compassion reserves increase.

Even in the writing of this book, as I think about things that I can do to build up my compassion reserves, the actual writing process is a behavior that helps me in that area. By sharing experiences or wisdom or knowledge from my life or those around me, I am able to build up my compassion reserves. We naturally find it easier to be more compassionate to others when those around us have shown compassion to us. Compassion has a kind of ripple effect.

As we share compassion reserves, the ripple effect of giving to others bounces back onto ourselves. It is important to take account of the level of your reservoir. Be aware of your compassion reserve and constantly look for ways to refill your reservoirs. When we do this, we become healthier individuals and are better able to be compassionate to others.

WSC

Living in the Redline

Health care burnout may often lead to compassion fatigue, anxiety, substance abuse, depression, and suicide.

Common symptoms of work "burnout" include anxiety, depression, irritability, feeling tired even after resting (chronic fatigue), cutting back on leisure activities, resentment, difficulty concentrating, and neglecting responsibilities.

These facts should set off alarm bells for the medical profession as a whole, as well as the public. Like a canary in a coal mine, these symptoms warn us of a general increase in disabling anxiety conditions as a whole among the general population. Currently we are seeing epidemic levels of work-related post traumatic stress disorder (PTSD) in all health care providers, such as policemen, firemen, and ambulance paramedics.

Some symptoms of PTSD may include nightmares, intrusive thoughts recalling the traumatic event, flashbacks, efforts to avoid feelings and thoughts that either remind you of the traumatic event or that trigger similar feelings, and feeling detached or unable to connect with loved ones.

PTSD, however, is not limited to frontline health care workers. It is a common psychological defense mechanism seen in people who have suffered high-intensity physical and/or psychological injury. The PTSD response acts to prevent similar circumstances from occurring again, and it is arguable protective for the person, despite being associated with intense situational anxiety and fear.

I see PTSD frequently in people who have suffered chronic physical pain or injury from a motor vehicle accident. These individuals will experience serious anxiety symptoms as a driver or passenger of a car, or even being near a highway or road. PTSD is a relatively common diagnosis today as awareness of its symptoms have grown within the medical profession and general public.

The worldwide opioid crisis is commonly reported in the media, with lethal overdose a far too common complication. What most people don't know is that many opioid users are doing so as a method of self-medicating untreated chronic physical and/or emotional pain. The opioid epidemic is seemingly not well understood by the governing bodies. It is, in fact, not related specifically to doctors prescribing opioids. Rather, it is more closely tied to a progressive escalation of our societies' growing anxieties, with no means to manage the emotional and physical pain of modern life.

I have studied, researched, and worked in the area of complex interventional pain and rehabilitation medicine for nearly twenty-five years. From a physical perspective, even twenty-five years ago, I was seeing people working and playing or competing beyond the range of the physical abilities of their bodies. This physical overuse caused them to develop chronic myofascial pain, neck and spinal pain and injury, many forms of tendonitis, and various pain syndromes both simple and complex, all leading to physical disability.

Twenty-five years ago, repetitive strain injury (RSI) became a concern as neck and arm pain syndromes were on the rise, due to chronic repetitive activity being increased both on the factory line and in the office. The use of computers and their mice place us in awkward body positions, creating neck and upper limb injuries that are very difficult to treat and can and do lead to permanent physical disability. Computer-related RSI has become a household name, and the condition has spread to other devices such as smartphones, computer gaming devices, sitting positions, and even sleeping positions.

Fibromyalgia was medically described by the American Rheumatology Association in the early 1990s, and it was estimated to affect 2 percent of the population at that time. Like burnout, PTSD, and RSI, these estimates need a major revision, with true numbers being much higher than originally estimated. In the pain community, I believe that at least 30 percent of the population is living with chronic pain. Chronic pain such as low back pain, migraines, RSIs, muscle pain, and joint pain represent 50 percent of all medical visits in North America and Europe.

Our kids are not unaffected. A 2017 American study of children reported the use of smartphones for more than two hours a day caused major sleep effects, fatigue, and school performance issues.

Further, the words *efficiency, modernization, downsizing,* and *competitive edge* are creating impossible work environments.

Today, I see everyone living in what I call "the redline." I use this term to describe a physical state similar to an automobile with a small engine being driven too hard; the RPMs of the engine are constantly running too high for its design.

In the auto industry, we are seeing small engines being turbocharged not once but twice, so as to deliver more power using less gasoline, in order to achieve more efficient gas mileage. The auto industry is also reporting record-level engine failure in these over-revved small engines. Many industry insiders say there is no replacement for engine displacement; that is, appropriately sized motors for the power delivered.

In the same way, our bodies and minds are constantly running too hot and revving too high, causing signs of cracking and failure. Individuals have responded to these demands and injuries by consuming record levels of over the counter, prescription, and illegal medication for pain and anxiety, all in an effort to manage the symptoms of both physical and psychological failure.

Quite simply, we are not designed to run this fast and hard and stressed all the time. The fight-or-flight response was designed to be an emergency, life-saving, adrenaline-charged response. It was meant to be both unique and rare—not a way of life for everyday activity and work. Twin-turbo-charged people living in the redline will typically burn out, and they may not recover physically or mentally.

To function properly, humans all need these basic things:

- normal, healthy sleep patterns
- regular, reasonable exercise consisting of stretching, resistance training, and mild to moderate aerobics
- reasonable work hours
- family time
- partner time
- holiday time
- a safe, happy work environment
- a sustainable healthy diet

We also deserve some compassion and forgiveness for our mistakes and misgivings, not excessive criticism by coworkers, or worse, social media. A learning and supportive work environment helps the workers learn from their mistakes and not be forced to hide them. We need the promise of a longer-term commitment from society to the individual.

I won't pretend to have the answers to our society's modern problems. As a medical doctor treating physical pain and stress injuries, I am concerned about how our society does not seem to have the awareness and/or commitment to change our future path in physical and mental health. We cannot continue to live in the redline and expect anything but burnout. Make the choices you can to stay below the redline for a sustainable career and a satisfying life.

GBL

Finding Satisfaction

In a book that focuses on compassion fatigue, it is important to include a chapter on understanding what satisfies us. Finding satisfaction is often an ongoing process that starts in infancy and continues until we die. We must each take some time and identify what specifically satisfies us. This is helpful when trying to balance the rigors of caring for others with properly caring for ourselves. If we do not have some self-care habits in place, it is impossible to be effective in caring for others. Finding true satisfaction in life can take many years. It is sometimes very easy to identify what dissatisfies us but perhaps more difficult to identify what really provides satisfaction.

Finding satisfaction sometimes involves the process of going down different pathways in life and finding that this is not it. We then regroup and go down another pathway. I tend to think that the ultimate satisfaction in our lives has to deal with the spiritual component. By believing in something bigger than ourselves, we realize that ultimately the things that we typically seek out for satisfaction really do not provide it.

It is very common in our society to seek out things for satisfaction. Maybe certain clothes or a certain house or furniture or even a specific breed of dog. We chase many things in life, hoping that they will provide satisfaction. Many times when we have enough money to purchase the things we want, once we actually get those things, we find that they do not truly satisfy us. Satisfaction occurs at a very deep level of our souls. I tend to think that most of our satisfaction in life comes from our relationships. When we establish and maintain friendships and family relationships, this is part of the key to finding satisfaction.

I do not think, especially as we get older, that we tend to find satisfaction in acquiring things. Rather, satisfaction occurs with what is really important. Satisfaction occurs with having enough time to rest and reflect on life. Satisfaction does not occur by running ourselves ragged with our busy work schedules and personal commitments. Many times we are working too much or getting too caught up in busyness, and we actually avoid what would really be more satisfying to us. There are those who find exercise to be very satisfying. Perhaps they enjoy obtaining a record in an athletic event or participating in some type of difficult fitness activity. Since good health is part of being satisfied, then it would be only natural that we would find satisfaction in achieving physical goals.

For those who find satisfaction in obtaining educational degrees, it can be very rewarding to study hard and earn a high school degree or a college degree or even a graduate degree. With more education, many doors can be opened up for you, and these new opportunities can provide a sense of satisfaction. There are those who find satisfaction in their chosen professions or careers. For them, helping others is truly satisfying. Those who just focus on themselves tend to be very dissatisfied with life. Satisfaction occurs when we spend the time to help other people, when we give up thinking of ourselves and instead think of others.

I personally find satisfaction in exotic overseas travel. It satisfies me because I enjoy the planning process of the trip, the journey, and of course, the destination. It is very satisfying for me to have a travel goal, to work hard saving the money to pay for the trip, and then to actually go on the trip to see rare and unique animals. For me, that provides a sense of satisfaction.

What is truly satisfying to me is my friendships and other relationships that have occurred along the way in life. I find satisfaction in life when I am struggling and someone reaches out to care for me or offer a prayer of support or do something that affirms me. Satisfaction for me is not always limited to giving to other people; there is also a sense of satisfaction when someone acknowledges me and gives back to me.

Everyone needs to seek out what truly satisfies them and develop pathways to reach satisfaction in life. I know that there are those reading this book who get a true sense of satisfaction in life from their spiritual journey—their journey of assessing something bigger than ourselves. Ultimately those experiences can be very satisfying.

In summary, I tend to think that satisfaction lies in relationships. Satisfaction is not typically found in the acquisition of things. Take time to enjoy your life. Take time to reflect on your life. Do not work all of the time and miss out on satisfaction in your life. Even if your job is satisfying, take time out of your busy schedule and identify those things that truly satisfy you. Spend more time investing in relationships around you. Invest in a relationship with God, with family, and with friends. I truly believe that ultimately, that will be a satisfying experience for you.

Healthy Hormones

In their drive to care for others, caregivers often neglect caring for themselves. Even when the body is sending you warning messages, the warnings go unheard and unheeded. One of the measures of health is our hormones. Stressful careers and lives can stress our hormones, too. Those stresses can rob us of the important and protective role that our hormones play in our overall health and wellness.

Throughout the day, the body's demands for each hormone change. Your body reacts to what is happening in your life. Hormones are delivered into the bloodstream to cells in various tissues. The hormones bind to a specific cell receptor, like a key fitting into a particular lock. Once this binding takes place, there is a biological effect. This effect can be either positive or negative. An example of a good effect is the hormone testosterone binding with a receptor in the skin and causing growth of hair on the chin, or that same hormone binding to a cell in the testes to produce sperm.

If there is a negative effect, it can stop the production of a substance. The production of hormones is regulated by a delicate set of feedback loops. This means that the amount of the substance in the system regulates its own concentration. When there are low levels of a hormone, there is positive feedback, and more of that hormone is produced. However, when hormone levels get to the appropriate level, there is negative feedback, and production of that hormone stops. This is very much like a thermostat on the wall regulating temperature. These balances are very delicate and can be changed by chemicals, stress, and injury.

Since the pituitary gland and the hypothalamus are located near or in the brain, traumatic brain injuries (TBI) can cause hormone problems. The TBI may change hormone production right away, or it can affect hormone levels years, and even decades, after the injury. I also have seen many examples in my practice where severe stress greatly affects hormone levels. Post-traumatic stress disorder (PTSD) is a typical example of this.

In summary, optimal hormone levels are critical for health and well-being.

Concussions, other brain injuries, and PTSD can upset this fine balance and lead to illness and deterioration of health.

However, the hopeful message is that we are now recognizing these hormone abnormalities. When we can optimize hormone levels, those suffering can improve significantly, and some may even get better completely.

Life is a roller coaster, and certainly your hormones reflect this.

After you were born and while you were young, optimal hormone levels were necessary for you to grow and develop correctly. This is particularly important for the brain. This incredibly complex organ has to develop connections for forming memories and allowing you to learn tasks and skills. The brain is also the control center of the body and maintains vital activities, such as programming your heart to beat and your lungs to breathe and your muscles to work.

Substances like growth hormone and thyroid hormone are critical in childhood development. There are many other hormones playing an important role. If these hormones are not optimal, normal development can be a problem.

As puberty is reached, the sex hormones (estrogen and progesterone in the female and testosterone in the male) are responsible for sexual development. In girls, this causes the development of breasts and pubic hair, the growth of the uterus, and maturation of the ovaries that starts menstrual periods. In boys, this causes development of the penis, the growth of hair on the body, the deepening of the voice, and the strengthening of muscles.

There are also considerable changes within the brain that lead to the development of sex drive and the changes in emotions that occur as adolescents grow. Once this development has taken place, levels of hormones tend to stabilize.

However, in women, this so-called stability still includes monthly changes in hormones. There are volcanic eruptions of estrogen. Blood levels during the day the menstrual period starts are at around 27 pg/mL (100 pmol/L), increasing to 436 pg/mL (1600 pmol/L) at ovulation some two weeks later, and then falling back down over the next two weeks. This 1,600 percent increase in hormones can cause incredible changes in feelings and moods.

In men, testosterone levels are reasonably stable in the healthy individual.

They go higher with mild exercise but can be depressed by extreme exercise, such as training for a marathon or undergoing conditions of stress.

Women come to a time in life called perimenopause. This is characterized by changing hormone levels. As the ovaries wear down, they are no longer fine-tuned. They are instead somewhat unpredictable.

Menstrual periods may continue to be regular, or they may start becoming irregular. As early as when a woman reaches her mid-thirties, she may complain of menopause-like symptoms, such as hot flashes and sweats. Women are often told this cannot happen, but indeed it does. The symptoms are caused by hormone levels dipping below the optimal range, at some point in the cycle. During the rest of the cycle, the hormone levels may return to normal. In other cases, the hormone levels may shoot too high and cause symptoms of fluid retention and breast tenderness.

As men age, they can see some reduction in their hormone levels. This may exhibit with symptoms of fatigue, sleeplessness, loss of muscle, and mood changes like irritability, depression, or decreased sex drive.

Menopause occurs when the ovaries run out of eggs and hormone levels of estrogen and progesterone plummet. Menopause is defined as having no menstrual periods for one year. The average age of menopause is 51, with a normal range of 45 to 55.

Menopause may include any or all of the following symptoms:

- Hot flashes
- Night sweats
- Poor memory
- Poor mood
- Poor concentration
- Poor energy
- Vaginal dryness
- Bladder not working well
- Irritability (the risk of which triples in menopause)
- Depression (the risk of which also triples)
- Joint pain and muscle ache (the only symptom that occurs in 100% of women with very low estrogen)
- Sleep disturbance
- Decreased sex drive

- Palpitations of the heart
- Headache
- Weight gain
- Brain fog (since blood flow to the brain drops 30 percent and 26 areas in the brain which require estrogen and progesterone are not getting them)

Your menopausal "computer" has 30 percent less power and 26 fewer programs to run. No one likes this computer!

But symptoms are not the greatest problem. There is also an increased risk of serious chronic fatal illness. The risk of stroke and heart attack goes up considerably, with 54 percent of menopausal women dying of these vascular problems. There are also increased risks of diabetes, bowel cancer, osteoporosis, Alzheimer's disease, dementia, and breast cancer.

Restoration of hormones identical to human hormones (bio-identical hormones) reduces these risks considerably. Some calculations put the reduction in deaths each year with hormonal restoration at 29 percent. (This topic will become the subject of a later book we are writing.)

Men encounter a similar but not so obvious condition. There is nothing such as the loss of menstrual periods to mark the onset of problems.

The signs are usually much more subtle. This condition is called Andropause or Low Testosterone Syndrome.

Symptoms of low testosterone may include the following:

- Fatigue
- Sleep disturbance
- Loss of muscle and joint pain

- Headache
- Pounding heart
- Hot flashes or sweats
- Development of more breast tissue
- Weight gain around the middle
- Anxiety, anger, or depression
- Loss of competitive drive
- Poor memory
- Shying away from social gatherings
- Loss of confidence
- Erectile dysfunction and/or poor sex drive
- Loss of enjoyment of life

As it is with women in menopause, loss of testosterone in men can lead to large increases in stroke, heart attack, diabetes, Alzheimer's disease, depression, and arthritis, among other conditions. These can be significantly decreased with hormone-replacement therapy. (This topic is the subject of yet another book that we are writing.) However, what is critical to know is that concussions, brain injuries, and PTSD can depress these hormones and lead to these symptoms appearing in men and women prematurely.

This can happen at any age.

As a matter of fact, many of the symptoms of post-concussion syndrome are identical to the symptoms of low sex hormones in men and women.

Restoring hormone levels in these individuals can improve or eliminate the symptoms, improve their health immediately, and decrease chronic illness down the road.

Other hormones may fall as life goes on. In particular, in women, the thyroid hormones are often suboptimal, and this problem needs correction for best health.

If you are in the helping professions or serving as a first responder, caring for your health includes caring for your hormones too. See your health care professionals to learn what will help you to be your healthiest you.

LDK

Don't Go Swimming Alone

At the age of eight, one of my first great adventures outside of my family circle was going to summer camp. For me, this first camp experience was at Forest Cliff Camp, located on the eastern shores of Lake Huron, north of Sarnia, Ontario. Like many church camps, Forest Cliff was founded in the 1930s.

The property at the time included cabins for the junior campers and wood-framed bases with tent tops for those who were in middle school and high school. Sports included baseball, soccer, croquet, tetherball, and capture the flag. There was horseback riding, archery, crafts, and many other activities to expand your range of experiences. Many badges could be earned during the two weeks. Sometime during the session, we would always go on hunts with our pillow cases for the elusive and imaginary "snipe." Ah, the many ways counselors would find to ensure the campers were tired out, so all could have a good night's sleep!

Central to the camp was the campfire. There, we would sing songs, hear stories, and experience a real sense of community. As it was a Christian camp, we also heard about awakening our sense of wonder for the spiritual dimensions of life, including Bible stories and ideals for living a meaningful life. Some of these camp leaders who volunteered their summer vacations to enhance the lives of children would become important influences for years to come. For me, one of the camp directors, Jim Sparks, continues to be a friend fifty years later. Many friendships were also forged with fellow campers from different cities who shared a cabin during those formative years.

While many camps have a swimming pool to relieve the heat of summer and to learn how to swim, we could swim in a pool that was a Great Lake. Blessed with a long and white sandy shoreline, we enjoyed sandcastles and games on the beach. The lake provided us both calm and wavy days to venture out in old, cedar canoes that could hold seven or eight of us.

The swimming area had a shallow, sandy bottom that gradually grew deeper until it was about four feet deep. The waves could add a foot to that, depending on the wind that day. The boundaries were set each year using the lifeguard stands and ropes that were put out into the water, according to the depth that year. The water could be very chilly for those of us on the waterfront staff in mid-June when we would venture out to set up the swimming area!

While some July mornings could be as smooth as glass, by the time campers were ready for morning waterfront activities and swimming lessons, and usually by the afternoon swim for all the camp family, the waves were up. Like most of the lower Great Lakes, the clarity of the water decreases once the waves start whipping up the bottom. Visibility is poor.

Once I became one of the waterfront staff, and later as the Waterfront Director, I understood that if someone disappeared under the water, it would be difficult to notice him. Our lifeguards were all well trained, but like everything, you have to adapt your general training to the specifics of the area you are supervising. That meant that we had a special focus on monitoring each of the campers, in a different way than you would in a pool setting. We did that by using the "buddy system."

Before any of the campers could go in the water, they had to check in to the beach station with their numbered tag and with a buddy. Both tags were placed on a hook together. From that moment on, each of the campers had a responsibility to not enter or leave the water without their buddy being with them. As they played in the waves or enjoyed the other water activities, they had to always know where their buddy was. If they could not see their buddy, they had to call out to one of the lifeguards nearby immediately. Then everyone would stop, and a headcount would begin to ensure everyone was with their partner. The missing buddy would be spotted and reunited, with the reminder for everyone to keep their eyes on each other.

This did not replace the work of the lifeguards, but it added another layer of protection for the campers. They each became additional eyes and ears to ensure everyone was safe. If there was a problem spotted, they could call for help. When it came to their buddy—they were connected for the entire time that they were in the water until they together left the beach and checked out with the beach station.

That same principle of the "buddy system" is valuable for those in the caring professions as well. Who is a colleague who has his professional eyes on you, to ensure that you are okay? Who is paying attention to how you are coping with the stresses and demands of your work? Who will be able to warn you when they see you getting in over your head?

In moments of crisis, young swimmers do not always know to call out for help. They can panic. In the camp on a northern lake, swimmers used the dock to jump into the water. It was not a shallow bottom that allowed you to wade out. Campers were tested to ensure that they had the swimming skills to safely be in this deeper water. On one occasion, I was the lifeguard, and as I surveyed the small group that was swimming, my eyes focused on a swimmer who had a terrified look on his face. He was in over his head, and for whatever reason, had lost his confidence.

He did not cry out or wave his arms. But I knew, as I looked into his eyes, that he was in trouble. I jumped in and pulled him out, and he rested on the dock. He later told me that he just got scared and thought he was going to drown.

The same can be true of our colleagues and of us, too. Sometimes, we know that we are trouble and can reach out. Other times, we panic, and no words come out as we begin to succumb to the pressure. As caregivers, our focus on others can also lead us to not declare our emergency, since others need us to carry on. That's when a buddy can reach out to us and help us get back to a safe depth. Those who have had the benefit of knowing their team members longer are able to detect those early warning signs before the danger increases. They can see the changes in your mood, the way you handle the everyday tasks of your role, and how you are coping with the pressures around you.

This "buddy" role is different than that of a supervisor in your organization who would have responsibilities as your leader. They, too, should be paying attention to how you are doing, and it is wise to keep them updated on how you feel work is going. But because they are in that senior role, you may also benefit from having a peer (someone who is in a similar role to yourself) as your buddy.

If your role is that of a sole practitioner, find a colleague who will agree to check on you and you on them with a phone call, an e-mail, or a cup of coffee.

Having a mutual commitment to keep an eye on each other can be very reassuring, even when things are going well. Many people who have faithfully served others as caregivers unexpectedly find themselves as the person in crisis. They can drown in the swirling and churning waters of taking care of clients, patients, and the public.

Don't go swimming alone—check in with a buddy. Together, you will protect yourself, your family, your career, and the people you are serving.

GDF

Stepping Back from the Edge

How do we know when it's time to either call it quits or to pull in the reins on our efforts? That tends to be a personal observation that each individual must make for themselves. Many times, we get so caught up in caring for others that we quit caring for ourselves. When we do this consistently and do not take care of ourselves appropriately, we end up burned out, depressed, anxious, or frustrated. In other words, we wind up at the edge. What does the edge look like? It can look like fatigue, it can look like despair, it can look like frustration, and it can look like all of these at once. When you find yourself at the edge, it's time to step back and look for your oasis.

When we realize that we have given and given and given until we are consistently tired, frustrated, or burned out, we must pull the reins in, regroup, and refill our reservoirs. What does pulling back look like when you reach the edge?

Maybe you look at your schedule for the week and see that you're double booked or overly committed, so that you don't have time for yourself or your family or friends. Maybe you've allocated so much time to caregiving—whether for a sick parent, a close friend, a loved one, or perhaps even a patient—that you are so tired and worn out that you can't go on. Stepping back from the edge might mean that we take ourselves off certain committees at church or that we volunteer at fewer organizations or perhaps attend fewer social events. It might mean that we don't see clients or patients after 5:00 p.m. on weekdays and keep weekends to ourselves.

If we must work on weekends, for whatever reason, we may find that we need to take off a day or two during the week to compensate for our caregiving. Stepping back from the edge is essential to taking care of ourselves. This is not an optional behavior. Many times, it is absolutely necessary so we're not drawn into the fire. Stepping back from the edge might include turning off your cell phone after a certain time or not responding immediately to text messages or e-mails. It might involve eliminating time with those who drain our energies and damper our spirits. It might involve clarifying boundaries with your office personnel or your coworkers.

Your family might also need to have clarification of boundaries so that you can regroup and energize yourself and be the person that you need to be. Sometimes our pride is the driving factor in our caregiving. Sometimes our ego is such that we only feel good about ourselves if we work ourselves to oblivion or if our schedule is completely booked day in and day out. It's important to recognize that in ourselves and then take care of ourselves by doing what is necessary to repair the damage that can occur when our ego runs unchecked. Having a strong ego is not necessarily bad, but it can lead us down dangerous pathways that cause us to feel like we are about to go over the cliff.

If we feel like we are at the edge or over the edge, we might need to confide in a close friend or clergy member or mental health professional to guide us back to reality and back to a calmer lifestyle. Other ways to pull back might be taking a retreat or a vacation, or perhaps substituting more relaxing activities for scheduled hours of caregiving. Whatever you need to do to pull back from the edge, do it. Please take care of yourself, and don't be dependent on the opinions of others around you.

Our culture and perhaps many of our friends and family view us only when we're working and comforting others or being compassionate towards those in our care. Many times we are fearful to pull back from the edge because of the reactions of our family and friends. We might be afraid of the reactions of those in our parish or congregation or clinical practice. We might worry about the reaction of our coworkers if we are not exhibiting workaholic behaviors. You must lay all these fears aside and do the right thing to protect yourself, so that you can be a source of compassion for others, both now and for years to come.

We are human, and we are not able to be compassionate 100 percent of the time.

We need to pull in the reins, step back, look at our lives, and regroup so that we don't go over the cliff.

WSC

Bouncing Back

Stressful situations stretch us. That can be great if it is a stress that challenges us to do something new or explore our limits. Long-term stress can have a different result. It can cause us to experience a number of negative side effects. Sleep becomes more difficult. Anxiety may rise when we approach that workplace where we feel overwhelmed. Blood pressure can go up. Depression can set in.

You will find yourself stretched quickly by a crisis. All your energy, skills, concentration, and even physical resources are called upon to deal with what is happening at that moment. The crisis passes. Then you begin to return to normal.

Depending on how often these crises occur, you might return to your shape quickly or more slowly. Like anything that is stretched, if it is stretched too often or too quickly, there is a great risk of a tear or a leak.

Sustained stress has a different dynamic. You do not have the rapid rise and fall of an urgent crisis, but you exist at a higher level all the time. This changes many of your dynamics physically, emotionally, mentally, socially, and spiritually. Many of our human systems are equipped well for a short-term stress response. Chronic and persistent stress takes a different toll. It begins to change us. That in turn, changes our view of ourselves, our work relationships, and our life outside of work.

There are stresses that help us grow and develop as people. Any new situation, no matter how worthwhile, can be stressful. When we try to do something for the first time, we are uncertain. When we push ourselves to attempt something that is not easy for us, this can create stress. But ultimately those experiences can be positive. They create a good stress.

However, when our work keeps us stressed constantly with little or no relief, we increase the risks associated with compassion fatigue and burnout.

When you buy a carpet, one of the qualities in the material that distinguishes a good carpet from a great one is memory. As the salesperson will tell you, a carpet with a good memory will look great longer and be much more durable than a cheaper product that has a poor memory. What this means in the flooring business is that a well-constructed carpet, made of superior materials, will return to its shape quickly and reliably. If you walk on it, the carpet depresses. When you step off it, the spot will return to its familiar look. Poorer quality carpets take a long time to regain their height and texture. They become matted.

When you leave a heavy chair or table foot on the same spot for a long time, the carpet will develop a flat look underneath the weight of the object. As you move the furniture to a different spot, you may have an area that looks like something was there. Even a carpet that is of high quality can lose its memory, if the weight on it continues without relief for a long time.

This is true for caregivers as well. Your ability to bounce back and be your old self is affected by the pressures you are under. A brief experience can be recovered from quickly. However, if the pressure is constant and significant in the work you are doing, you could find yourself looking and feeling very different than you did before.

Some of the ingredients that give us a "good memory" include our personality, education, life experiences, self-esteem, physical health, and social vitality. These aspects of preparation and suitability for the role can help ward off burnout.

Yet even those with a great predisposition, suitable personality, and useful education are not immune to the damage of long term stress.

Beware the role that keeps you under chronic stress. These months and years of relentless demands and high expectations will take their toll on you and those in your world. Ultimately, it will lead you to be less effective as a caregiver. You may end up resenting your workplace, those in your care, your family, and even yourself.

Protect yourself by ensuring that your caregiver role includes sufficient support. Commit yourself to other activities that will refresh you and help you maintain a positive work/life balance.

Have a trusted colleague, friend, or family member "read the carpet" to see how well you are returning to shape. If that dent seems to be persisting, make some changes or engage in some of the strategies found elsewhere in this book.

It's okay to admit that it has been a heavy time and that you are feeling crushed. Recognize it. Make the short-term and long-term adjustments needed so you can bounce back!

GDF

Seasoned Travelers

Erik Erikson is well-known in the field of mental health as the specialist who has defined different stages of psychosocial development. Generativity versus stagnation is the seventh stage of Erikson's theory of psychosocial development. This stage typically takes place during middle adulthood between the ages of approximately 40 to 65.

As we all get older, we find that we have an innate desire that comes deep within us to help others that are younger than ourselves. We may find that that occurs with our children or grandchildren. There are those of us reading this book who perhaps do not have children or grandchildren and find themselves in relationships with younger individuals through their jobs or their ministries or other family relationships. Perhaps there is a niece or nephew that this concept would apply to. Whatever the case, this desire to pass along our accumulated knowledge occurs naturally during the aging process.

In the medical profession, generativity might come in treating younger patients and giving them guidance and direction for the future. It might occur when a physician teaches medical students or interns or residents because, consciously and unconsciously, she knows that they represent the next generation. There is a natural desire to contribute to the betterment of those who will come after us during this phase of our lives.

Generativity also occurs in the classroom, perhaps when a teacher recognizes that what she is teaching will have an impact on the next generation. The imparting of information or data or feelings all contribute to what the next generation will be like.

I am an individual who does not have biological children or grandchildren, but I still feel and am aware of this stage of social development in my life. I have been a big participant in physical fitness over the years, as I know how important that is for both mental health and physical health. I have been able to make time for personal training and physical fitness, including basic workouts as well as CrossFit training.

My trainers tend to be in their twenties and thirties, and I find myself becoming older and older in relationship to my trainers. As anyone is aware if they have been in exercise training, there is a very strong bond that develops between the trainer and the client. The bond works both ways. There is a sense of the young trainer, who is in a different stage of psychosocial development, giving to the client, but there is also a sense of generative mentoring that occurs either consciously or unconsciously as the older client gives back to the young trainer. The older individual does not want the younger individual to perhaps make the same mistakes that he made along the way when he was that age. The older individual, although not as physically spry as the trainer, does have a lot to offer in the area of life experience and wisdom that someone in an earlier stage of psychosocial development cannot appreciate at the time.

As we age, it is important that we engage and establish relationships with the generation that will come after us. This can be incredibly rewarding emotionally, physically, and spiritually. By helping and mentoring younger individuals, we end up helping ourselves. It gives us a sense of well-being and helps us as we move forward into the eighth stage of psychosocial development, which is integrity versus despair. If we do not mentor and engage in relationships with the younger generation, we will end up with a level despair in the eighth stage of psychosocial development.

In the context of caregivers experiencing weariness, a balance must be struck. Even though we need to invest ourselves into the lives of younger individuals, we still have to maintain our boundaries so that we do not become burned out, depressed, or anxious. Boundaries are discussed in another chapter, but they are important even with regards to this concept. Maintaining appropriate boundaries helps us be the best mentors and role models for the generation that comes after us. To do this, we must take a look at ourselves closely and make sure that we are taking care of ourselves in order to take care of others.

WSC

The Power to Care

When we say that we care for someone or are showing care for someone, what does that mean? Perhaps we are feeling concerned about that person, worried about that person, or interested in that person's life struggles. This chapter will deal with the word *caring* as a verb. Caring is not action that is carried out by individuals in a deliberate, intentional manner. The title of this chapter, "The Power to Care," implies that it takes a lot of energy or power to care about someone in their situation. Are we strong enough to care about someone else today?

When we care about another individual, it means that we need to put our own problems, schedules, and busyness behind so that we can give that person the importance, time, and interest that they need. Caring for others is more natural for some of us than it is for others. As we talked about in other chapters, caring might seem easier if you work in a job that is known as a "caring profession," such as the ministry or the medical field.

We all have the capacity to care for one another, wherever we are at that point in time. We do not have to be in a specific profession, a specific place, or a specific context to care for others. Caring might include what seems a simple act to us, but it comes across as a very life-changing experience for the recipient of our care. Caring for others might involve praying for them, perhaps when we cannot be physically present with that person that we want to care for.

Feeling strong enough to care about another person implies that we have the emotional energy and/or physical energy to execute the process of caring. We tend to get complacent in our daily world and many times not step outside our box to care for others. We need to wake up with a consciousness of caring. There are always others who need our help and assistance. As we have discussed in other chapters, though, we need to be able to set boundaries for ourselves so that we have the capacity and power to care for others. If we give too much, we put ourselves in danger of becoming burned out, depressed, or physically ill. To be able to feel strong enough to care for others today, we have to take care of ourselves also.

I hope that we can all think of many times in our lives when others have taken the time to care for us—when someone else has recognized our need to being cared for and has reached out to do that for us. Many caregivers experience great fulfillment and joy when they give to others, but the recipient of that care is also joyful.

I would like to share a couple of memories from my life of times when someone cared for me. This might be perceived as a simple act, but it was very life-changing and memorable to this day. As I share these two stories of caring from others, try to think about times when you were able to be cared for by someone, or a situation in which you were able to care for others.

In the first case, imagine a young man who was visiting a close friend of his at a summer camp. His friend was a counselor at the camp, and he had traveled to visit him at the end of college. It was clear to the young man that this would probably be the last time he would see his friend for perhaps a very long time, as he was going to start graduate school and his friend was going to get married and move away. As this young man was realizing these facts of life, he sat down on the edge of a lake at the summer camp and started to weep. He was crying not necessarily about the loss of the friendship but about the loss of being able to see his friend in person on a regular basis and perhaps not being as close of a friend, as life has a way of doing that with us. We get caught up in the busyness of our jobs, our families, our own problems, our lives, and if we do not take the time to care for others and have the power to care for them, then those friendships generally go by the wayside. When this young man was sitting by the lake, another friend of his close friend came up and asked what was the matter. This young man shared what he was feeling, what was going on, and at that moment in time, this friend showed compassion and caring.

This friend had the power to care and obviously was strong enough to care for this young man that day. Even now, almost forty years later, the power of caring by that individual for the young man is remembered. It is possible that the friend who comforted the young man does not even remember what happened that day, but it was life-changing for the recipient of that caring.

Now imagine a young personal trainer caring for an older client. The trainer asked the older client how he was doing after a weekend, expecting to hear that things were fine or everything was great, but that is not what the trainer heard. He heard that his client was distressed, worried, and sad. His client was also confused about the future. The client said to the trainer that he did not expect the trainer to do anything, change the situation, or fix it, and the exercise session went on as planned. Nothing else was brought up during the exercise session about what the client had said. But at the end of the session, the personal trainer asked the older client to come outside the building where it was quiet and private. The trainer asked the older client if he would be okay if he prayed for him. The older client, somewhat surprised, willingly accepted the offer of prayer. The personal trainer prayed about the distress and concern that the older client was feeling. The older client felt very comforted by this younger personal trainer having the power to care and using that power and concern to show interest in what was going on with the client at the time.

The story above is a recent memory for me. It was a life-changing experience that occurred while I was in the middle of writing this book on compassion fatigue. My trainer would probably remember this act of caring, but he might not realize how powerful it was for me at the time. That is not uncommon. Many times our simple acts of caring can have profound impacts on those we care for. Be aware of others' needs and also share your needs with others. People cannot read our minds, know what is on our hearts, or guess what our needs are. Do not assume that someone else knows what is going on in your life and how you are feeling.

Be one who will care for others as well as be cared for. Develop your life so that you are strong enough to care for others today. There is incredible power in seeing people's needs and reaching out to help.

WSC

Caring for Special Children

It has been said that perhaps the most rewarding, and at the same time the most difficult, experience in life is having a special needs child. I am sure that there are many reading this book who either have a special needs child or have a family member or friend with a special needs child. "Special needs" can be a very broad term for a variety of disabilities that may include autism, intellectual disability, or physical disability, such as cerebral palsy.

The first thing is to be able to identify whether your child has special needs and what they are. To do this, you must interact with and observe your child from birth. Pay attention to the child's interaction with primary caregivers initially and later with other family and friends. You might become aware that your child has special needs early in life. You may notice that your special needs child does not behave or interact the same as another sibling did at that age.

If you notice that you might have a special needs child, do your best early on to get a proper diagnosis and appropriate medical attention, as well as psychological support. One of the most important things when having a special needs child is to interact with that child. Sometimes it is a natural tendency to not interact as much with a special needs child, because the interaction requires more energy and determination. Try not to avoid interacting with your special needs child, and if you are already doing this, be aware of your behavior and try to improve it. The other thing that is very important, especially early on, is to observe your child. Notice his or her feeding patterns, eating patterns, and behavior patterns. Notice the emotional expressions of your child. Use common sense when raising a special needs child. If you have raised children, you recognize how vital it is to be flexible. This is especially true with special needs children as sometimes their emotions and behaviors can be unpredictable.

One of the best behavioral techniques for children with special needs is to be consistent with boundaries. Set the boundaries early on and maintain them. Many times, raising a special needs child can be tiring; that is when we need to be consistent with our boundaries and not let our guard down. Children with special needs develop better with consistent boundaries. The boundaries need to be clear, and proper behavior should be rewarded. When boundaries are maintained, the special needs child needs to have consistent positive reinforcement. The single most important quality to raising a special needs child in the best way possible is to be positive with that child. Negativity can multiply itself with special needs children, and so being positive is essential.

When raising a special needs child, keep in mind the concept of parenting as a marathon, not a sprint. The special needs of your child will be there tomorrow and the next day and the next week and the next month. The child's abilities may improve with age and treatment, but we all need to be prepared for the long-term in this process. Those who have a sprint mentality will not be as effective in raising a special needs child. I am not saying it is easy; I am not saying it is always fun or emotionally rewarding. But one needs to focus on the marathon experience when raising a special needs child.

It goes without saying that raising a special needs child requires a plan. Work out this plan with your spouse or partner, if you have one, so that you both stay on the same page regarding consistency and boundaries and staying positive. You may be raising a special needs child on your own. Whether you are parenting on your own or with a spouse, it takes a village to raise a child. The village needs to be larger for special needs children. Early on you must establish networks of support in the medical field, the mental health field, and for those who are religiously inclined, the spiritual field. If you have a support network in place, someone can step in at those times when you are wary and discouraged and exhausted. Utilize your support system. Simply identifying your support system is not enough for raising a special needs child. Be in close contact with those you can count on for support—those who will be there when you need them to be there.

The safety drill at the beginning of every flight includes seat belts, signs, exits, flotation devices, and oxygen masks. Flight attendants always remind us that if the cabin loses pressure and the oxygen masks deploy, put your mask on first, before assisting others. That is good advice for all those who are caring for others. We must take care of ourselves to be in a position to help others.

Having a special needs child is an enormous challenge. It can be very rewarding and exciting, or it can be a source of depression and fatigue. Taking care of yourself first is essential, so that you are able to take care of your special need child. Identify and utilize your support systems— medical, psychological, and spiritual. By utilizing all your support systems, you have the best chance of continuity while raising a special needs child.

WSC

Lend Me Your Ear

One of the ways that we relieve stress is to talk.

For the caregiver, you may be in a role that includes a great deal of communication. The idea of more talking might seem strange to others outside of your world.

Venting is part of the job.

Over the course of the day, you may feel a persistent stress that comes from caring for the needs of others hour after hour. Repetition of the many daily tasks accumulates, so that by the end, you might wonder how you got through it. First-responders and others experience days that have spikes to them. Quieter moments may be interrupted by a crisis or a call that requires immediate action and intensity. The rush of adrenaline heightens the senses, but the helpful stress of the moment can linger well past the event.

There are also days when you experience the weird, amazing, or frustrating patient or client who creates one of the many stories that caregivers accumulate over their careers. If most caregivers recorded their collection of "Ripley's Believe It or Not!" in a book, it would need to go in the fiction section of the library. For those who are not doing what you do, it is hard to imagine that these strange tales could be true. You, however, have lived it.

Telling these stories and sharing your day is helpful to release some of the tension and energy that the day has created. Verbalizing the experiences allows you to both process the day and begin to put it in the past. The act of talking about what happened (past tense) at work today begins to create some distance from the stress, frustration, sadness, grief, or other emotions attached to the day.

Ask any spouse, partner, good friend, or other family member of a caregiver, and they will nod knowingly when the subject of venting is discussed. They are used to the phone call in which their loved ones may not wait for the question, "How was your day?" They will just start telling their stories. Perhaps it is the commuter call on the journey home. If not before, then those first moments at home soon become a time to regale the others present with your day's highlights and lowlights.

Like most things in life, this sharing time can be helpful to a point but can also be harmful, if we are not careful.

Of course, there are confidentialities in the workplace that must be maintained. It is easy to allow too many details to infuse the conversation. Those details are not necessary to gain the benefits of venting.

The family member or friend who is doing the listening needs to be considered as well. There are times when they are not up to the recitations at that moment. Caregivers need to pay attention to their listeners, who may have had their own challenges from their day or who may just be tired.

When the stories include events that have made you angry, be careful not to project the anger or frustration you are feeling onto your ally, who is trying to be there for you. Stress is transferable. Be sure you are not stressing someone else as you relieve your pressure.

Be purposeful to include some positive stories or moments from the day. There may be shifts when you may feel that you have to look high and low to find something good. Make the effort to find that bright spot and share it. That will make it easier on your listener, and it will remind you that your day was not all bad. Do not forget to ask your spouse or friend how their day was too. They may or may not have as stressful a role as yours, but others need to know that relationships are mutual and that you respect that.

When your designated listener (whether it is your significant other or a good friend) is also a caregiver, take the extra step to ask whether this is a good time to vent. You may also want to add some other close family or friends who are willing to lend you an ear to talk through your day.

If you really cannot discover anything good to share, start your next day at work with a commitment to look for something positive to remember. A role that truly includes nothing positive to retell at the end of the day suggests either a toxic workplace or a sign that you are becoming burned out.

It is true that some people want to finish work and just find an oasis of silence. This is especially true of introverts. They need to recharge their "quiet energy" so they can transition to their time outside the workplace.

Open the vents and breathe in the fresh air once again.

GDF

Bless Your Heart

As we help other people, many times we are rewarded emotionally and sometimes physically in the form of gifts. When we are in a helping profession or role, those receiving our help often express gratitude and applause for what we have done for them. It is important to recognize people's appreciation for us, but it is also important to maintain a balance.

This chapter involves the continual striving to maintain a balance between accepting gratitude and applause and giving to others. We need to examine our motives in giving. We need to look at our hearts and see why we are providing care for other people. Is it purely out of compassion? Or do we secretly crave their praise?

As noted in other chapters, caregiving includes many roles. We might be taking care of an elderly parent or working as a teacher or a minister or a medical professional. Many times, we get accolades from those we help and their families. We must be careful not to puff ourselves up and think that we are more than we are. We ought to feel thankful that we were able to serve other people. We need to show gratitude to those who appreciate our care. Always remember to acknowledge others when they reach out and say "thank you" or perhaps give some type of gift.

While we appreciate these words and gifts of gratitude, we must not live for the applause and recognition that we get from helping other people. We need to give simply because we care about others and we care about our role in helping others. When we start living for the applause, we tend to become prideful. Pride can blind us to what really needs to be done as we help other people.

Just as we talked about boundaries with other people and within ourselves in another chapter, we must also have a healthy boundary between caring for others and receiving and accepting their gratitude and thanks. Share with others that you appreciate the opportunity to be able to care for them or help them or serve them. Caring for others is a two-way street. We have noted in another chapter that if we spend too much energy caring for others and not taking care of ourselves, that we get burned out, and as a result, we can experience a variety of physical symptoms and emotional illnesses.

Maintaining a balance in your life is a very high goal that needs to be pursued. This requires frequent adjustments and recalibrations. We do not always have our lives in balance. Sometimes we are working too much or too hard, helping too many people, and in the process we hurt or neglect ourselves. When this happens, we must take a step back to avoid getting burned out.

There is nothing wrong with accepting gratitude and thanks for helping other people. The main issue is that this should not be our main motivating factor in providing care for others.

Helping others can give us a sense of well-being and joy. Sometimes when we see the challenges faced by those in our care, we can be thankful that we ourselves are not being challenged in that way. We can be thankful for our needs being taken care of. Yet many times we can get caught up in thinking that we are more than we are because of people's response to us. When we are in a caregiving profession or role, it is very common to get positive feedback on a regular basis. We might start to think we are this type of person when we are really another type of person. When we care for others, we have to examine our hearts and our motives. We need to maintain healthy boundaries. We need to acknowledge to the other person our gratefulness and thankfulness for their appreciation of our work and service, while remaining humbled at the same time. Humility in giving is really the virtue we need to strive for.

So, how do we accept gratitude in a healthy way? How do we not live for the applause? How do we recognize that people saying "thank you" to us as we serve them is important but not our reason for doing what we do?

Many of these questions that have been asked have different solutions or answers for each individual. The main thing is not to get prideful and to remain humble in your giving. That way, you can maintain a healthy balance in your life as you help other people.

WSC

PTSD

Many caregivers are exposed to physical risks as part of their service. First responders and those who serve in the military are at particular risk for concussions and other traumas. However, some who care for others in residential care, schools, nursing homes, hospitals, social work, and other settings also are at risk for injury. When these injuries include a concussion, PTSD may follow.

Post-traumatic stress disorder (PTSD) is common. It is estimated that more than 5 million people in the United States suffer from PTSD.

PTSD is defined as an anxiety disorder that can occur after a person has been through a traumatic event. Examples of such events can be car crashes, sexual or physical assaults, natural disasters, crimes, or combat during times of war. Typical of these events is a feeling that the person's life, or the lives of others, has been threatened. They feel that they have no control over the situation.

Not all people who go through these events get PTSD. Unfortunately, many do.

Here are some signs and symptoms of PTSD:

- Anxiety
- Irritability or outbreaks of anger

- Depression
- Nightmares
- Flashbacks
- Sleep disturbance
- Loss of positivity
- Physical responses to triggers of the traumatic event (such as an increased heart rate, a feeling of fear, or sweating)
- Avoidance of any people, places, or things that could trigger reminders of the event

It is important to note that many sufferers of PTSD also have had traumatic brain injuries. Recent research by Dr. Dewleen Baker, a psychiatrist at the University of California at San Diego, shows that traumatic brain injuries double the risk of PTSD. (You can read more about this research here: https://www.npr.org/sections/health-shots/2016/09/26/495074707/war-studies-suggest-a-concussion-leaves-the-brain-vulnerable-to-ptsd.)

As there is such an overlap of symptoms between traumatic brain injuries and PTSD, many of the treatments are similar. Often, patients receive cognitive behavioral therapy (CBT). However, I think that all organic causes need to be ruled out and treated first. This must include an accurate assessment of hormones, with a skilled interpretation of the results. The standard measure of hormones called "normal ranges" by labs is based on levels that include a large segment of the population. They certainly are not ideal or optimal levels; these are just what can be found in the general population. Hormones have to be restored and optimized to best levels, not settling for typical levels.

In addition, we know that many supplements can be helpful in treatment. (This is discussed in greater depth in a chapter on supplements in our book, *New Hope for Concussions, TBI & PTSD*.) Please note that Vitamin D is particularly useful. It has a major positive effect on mood and energy. The majority of patients I see have nowhere near ideal levels.

In PTSD, part of the problem is the inability to form new brain connections. For example, an event or an object linked to the original trauma that caused PTSD may continue to trigger bad memories. The reminder is very different from the actual event, but the body's response is the same. An example of this might be the sound like a siren that happened before a bomb blast. A siren heard long after the original event could still cause a fear response. The ability of the brain to form new memories in response to the siren may be impaired. Magnesium enhances the ability to form fresh nonthreatening memories. This allows the brain to be able to discriminate between the old existing memories of the siren and the new ones, so that the PTSD bodily response does not occur.

Unfortunately, PTSD is common in our troops and first responders. I have the greatest respect for the work that they do to keep us safe and healthy. That is why I am particularly delighted when I can help any of these brave individuals.

Much of what is written in the rest of this book is appropriate for treating individuals with PTSD. I want to continue our message of hope. This problem is not incurable; it can be treated.

Support groups are also very important. Sharing feelings and concerns with others who have gone through the same situation may reduce anxiety and fears. Family and friends are so important. Understand that those suffering from PTSD may withdraw. Those close to the PTSD survivors need to let them know that they will be there for them. Help them develop a network of family and friends who are willing to listen.

It is important that friends and relatives understand that individuals with PTSD may overreact in otherwise normal situations. They may suddenly become angry, and that anger may seem directed at their family and friends. These times are when caregivers and friends need to step back and realize that the anger is not really about them or anything they have done. This is a feature of the illness, and those around the sufferers need to have a high degree of tolerance and patience.

PTSD is as legitimate a diagnosis as appendicitis. We would never tell anyone with acute appendicitis to carry on with every activity of daily living. It makes equal sense that we should never tell someone suffering from PTSD that they should just "suck it up" and get on with their lives.

PTSD is an illness. It deserves our very best understanding and treatment solutions.

LDK

Survival Circle

We do many things to ensure our survival. There are the everyday choices we make to eat, drink, and exercise. We stay warm or cool as needed, and we look both ways before we cross the street. These are all important habits that we learn early and practice often in life.

Many other skills are added as we grow. We learn to read and write, though now perhaps not with phonics or with cursive. Our lives include relating to our family, friends, and the larger world around us.

Before long, we are taught what to do in an emergency. What happens if there is a fire? How do you call for help? Children must not talk to strangers. Learn to swim. Driver education will reduce your risks on the road.

Those who are in the caring professions, those who serve their community or country, and those who care for a loved one often miss another important survival technique. They have not formed their survival circle.

Giving, caring, listening, sharing, helping, teaching, calling, ministering, answering, serving—it is exhausting. You are the sponge that will be squeezed to provide a measure of relief for those in your care. A survival circle is one ingredient in protecting you from burnout.

In addition to professional support you engage regularly or in a crisis, creating a survival circle is a missed opportunity to support you in times of calm or chaos.

A survival circle is composed of friends to help you stay normal in the good times and sane in the bad times. In a crisis, they are the ones who are there to support you as a person.

Who do you choose?

You might be surprised to learn that the circle does not include people who are in your profession. Why not colleagues from work or friends in a similar career? People who do what we do understand what it is like. It is easy to exchange stories from your battlefield and to compare war wounds from being a caregiver. It is useful to have them in your story, but they will not be what you need for your survival circle.

When we share our stories with those who do what we do, we mentally and emotionally are still at work.

Instead, choose some compatible friends who are not part of your work life. By stepping outside of your professional life, you will have many more topics to discuss and enjoy. These more general friendships encourage you to think about the rest of your life's story. You may enjoy similar interests in sports, hobbies, movies, community or faith groups, travel, or the great outdoors. Like all great friendships, these deepen with the investment of time in each other. These relationships help you look away from the workplace when you are together. The risk of an all-consuming career is reduced because you have opportunities to explore life. That elusive work-life balance has the possibility of being discovered.

This is also helpful when you go through challenges in your career and life in general. These friendships give you someone to talk to about how it feels to be you at the various ages and stages of your journey. Of course, you will become a friend to them as well, encouraging them when the storms close in and celebrating the joys of life together as they happen.

How many of these friends should you have?

We recommend your survival circle to be eight people. Why so many when one or two are easier?

Surrounding yourself with a group of eight has a number of benefits. One of the risks as people grow older is that they concentrate on what is easy and convenient. It is easier and more convenient to have only two or three friends. But by making the effort to have a group of eight, you expand your range of experiences through these many relationships. Instead of just a mirror friendship where you enjoy everything the other person does, spending time with eight friends will create a more diverse group and will stimulate your life. That, in turn, makes you a more interesting person.

When life hits a rocky patch, spreading your need to talk or share about the challenges over a group of eight will ensure that no one or two friends will burn out when the heat is on. If you only have a few friends, those frequent calls to talk, times when you need to meet for a coffee, or other contacts can be overwhelming. That can lead to your few friends withdrawing in order to survive. More friendships spread the intensity of tough times and make your relationships sustainable.

Naturally, you will want to encourage your friends to have their own group of eight too. This will allow them to lean on the many, rather than the few, or the one. If you are a caregiver, you already know how people will be drawn to seek your time, support, and advice. When your days are already filled with listening, supporting, and being there for those in need, you cannot expect to be their only resource for survival.

Some of these friends will be closer to you than others in the group. Personality, history, and interests will influence that. However, choosing to reach out will pay off in the long run.

So, if we asked you today to name the friends who would be there for you in times of celebration or stress, who would they be? Who would make the list of those that you could call anytime to talk? Who would grab that cup of coffee or tea as needed? When something wonderful happens in your life, who would you tell? Who would want to know?

Some people are in our lives for a season. The important relationships that are often neglected are the friendships we hope will last a lifetime. These might include friends from our youth, college days, or some shared experience like a community project. You enjoy your time together, but you do not expect to be in touch over the many years ahead.

Other friendships have a quality or a shared experience that will endure the tests of life, distance, and time. Whether you see each other regularly or not, you can pick up where you left off comfortably, just as if you had never missed a moment. Treasure those relationships. They will sustain you and provide a sense of continuity as life is shaped and transformed with happiness and disappointments.

In our childhood, it is easy to make friends. As we age, it becomes more complicated. Once we have passed the stages of starting a career, entering a significant relationship, perhaps having children, and finding a community, we have to be more intentional to make new friendships. It is not as natural, and we are not as spontaneous as we once were. We become comfortable with what is known and what already is. And yet, throughout our lives, we will have people we will encounter who could enhance and enrich our stories. Does it occur to us that they might become our friends? Your assumption that they already have enough friends may cause you to miss out on a friendship that they might need and enjoy as well. Keep an open mind.

If you do not have eight on that list, start working on expanding your friendships. One way to do this is to ask, "Who would I want to be able to call a dear, old friend when I am retired?" Now is the time to invest in the relationships you will want to celebrate in the third act of your life story.

What's Burning?

Burnout is a common syndrome that occurs in individuals who are exerting more into their caregiving than their own resources allow. Burnout can be very gradual. It can creep up on us until it is almost too late. How do we know what burnout is? How do we know the warning signs? What do we do about it if we have burnout?

Burnout can manifest itself when we have spent too much energy and time in our jobs, working on a certain relationship, or caregiving for others. Burnout is common in many professional people, but it is not limited to that group at all. Burnout presents itself as a combination of psychological symptoms as well as physical problems. When one has spent too much time taking care of others, without an appropriate break, burnout may ensue.

Many of us have very strong wills and lots of endurance, and it takes a lot for burnout to hit us. There are others who are more fragile and more susceptible to burnout. It crosses all socioeconomic lines; it occurs in both men and women; it can occur in those living in the city, as well as those living in rural areas. Some of the physical symptoms of burnout might include extreme fatigue, headaches, nausea, and irritable bowel symptoms. Fatigue appears to be one of the most common symptoms associated with burnout.

There are a lot of different factors that contribute to fatigue, but that symptom in and of itself can indicate burnout. Fatigue may come from not sleeping well at night, or not getting enough sleep, or working long hours without an appropriate rest. Fatigue can occur from taking care of a patient, or taking care of someone in your congregation, or taking care of a family member.

Other physical symptoms include headaches, irritable bowel syndrome, and nausea. Headaches are very commonly reported with burnout. These can be quite severe. We know that migraine headaches are associated with burnout, as well as just with extreme exhaustion. Nausea, not feeling well, and general malaise are some symptoms that might tip us off to the fact that we are getting burned out. Many times when we are burned out, we do not eat appropriate foods. We do not exercise regularly. We may get extreme constipation, or diarrhea, or bloating. The body is naturally in tune with the mind, and if we are stressed out mentally, our bodies will be stressed out.

There are some mental characteristics that are associated with burnout. Psychologically, these may include anxiety and depression. Anxiety is an overwhelming sense of worry or fear that is with us on a regular basis. We may be anxious about our jobs or even perhaps losing our jobs. We might be anxious about our boss, or another coworker, or a client. Depression can also be a symptom of burnout. Depression is a syndrome of symptoms that include sleep disturbance, changes in appetite, fatigue, depressed mood, crying spells, and generally not wanting to do things. We know we are getting burned out when we dread going to work on a daily basis or when we are tired at work most or all of the time.

All of us need a break from our jobs as caregivers. None of us are superhuman. If burnout symptoms are severe enough, it is important to seek medical attention or mental health treatment.

If we have determined that we are suffering from burnout, what do we do? One of the first steps is to identify that we are burned out. After that, it is important to work on some solutions. Taking a break from work is a good way to start. This might include a few days off, or it might include an extended vacation. Do not discount the importance of recharging your batteries. When caregivers experience burnout, they might contemplate changing directions, getting a new job, or not caregiving as much in a certain role.

It is always important to set boundaries with ourselves and with others, so that we do not end up becoming burned out. Those who get burned out once are more likely to burn out again in the future, unless changes in schedules, jobs, or caregiving are made. In addition to getting some rest, we should talk to others about our burnout. Do not be isolated and bear the burden alone. Seek out a concerned friend, a pastor, a counselor, or a family member to let them know you are burned out and that you need some help in getting better.

More severe forms of burnout can require medicines for depression and anxiety. This might include some sleep medicines if your sleep cycles are severely disrupted. You might also begin some type of light exercise schedule, as we know that exercise can be quite helpful with burnout by increasing your energy levels. But be careful not to strain yourself doing too much exercise.

More severe forms of burnout can lead to a leave of absence from your job. This might even include hospitalization or a break away from family members who are causing you to be burned out. It is important that we take care of ourselves, so that we are able to care for others. Not setting boundaries with ourselves and others can many times lead to burnout. Try to set boundaries and set time for yourself, so that you can lead a happier life. Be aware of the warning signs of burnout before they get too severe. Help others with burnout if you have been helped yourself and are no longer in a state of burnout.

Burnout is an epidemic facing our society. With the advent of the Internet and instant accessibility, burnout is now more common than ever before.

Turn your cellphone off for a while. Do not check that e-mail every five minutes.

Allow yourself time to heal and rest.

Taking care of yourself will help you avoid burnout.

WSC

The Inside World

Caring for others can be a very rewarding task. Spending too much time caring can also be overwhelming and at times exhausting. Instinctively, human beings are designed to exhibit care for others. The extent to which one cares for other people can be determined a lot by genetics, environmental pressures, and work and personal schedules. There are those who have chosen to work in caring professions, such as being in the ministry or the medical field. There are many other types of occupations in which we can care for other people. When it comes down to it, we can be a stay-at-home mother or a retired postal worker or a nursing home resident and care for other people.

Caring for others is a process that seems to be both conscious and unconscious. Some of us are more naturally inclined to be able to care for other people, while for others it is more of an effort. Sometimes we need to schedule activities or appointments in our lives so that we are able to care for other people. Being there for others, especially in times of need, is one of the most important ways that we can care for other people. It is not necessarily what we say or what we do not say, but just our presence can communicate caring to other people. I think of times when perhaps we have lost a loved one or we are going through a financial stress or a relationship stress and someone steps in and cares. It can mean more to that person than you could possibly know.

What is happening inside of us as we care? We can look at biological changes that occur in the brain and nervous system that occur with caring. Changes in serotonin, dopamine, and oxytocin are all correlated with caring for other people. Sometimes these levels of neurotransmitters and hormones can be a contributing factor to a person's ability to care for others, or vice versa. Sometimes we change the levels of our neurotransmitters and hormones by caring for others. It is a generally accepted concept that when we do something kind for other people or care for other people, it helps us feel better about ourselves.

Caring for others can be self-preserving. Everyone is aware of the concept of karma. What goes around comes around. Perhaps caring for others will result in others caring for us. Yet we should not care for others expecting anything in return. Caring should be a selfless act of giving of ourselves, our time, and our finances. What actually goes on in our minds, in ourselves, in the process of caring? There is a sense of helping the other person, which causes us to have a better sense of well-being.

People who care for other people tend to live happier, more content lives. People who do not care for other people and remain focused on themselves tend to be more disgruntled with their lives and feel irritable and unhappy.

One of the overriding topics of this book is compassion fatigue. We do not want to give of ourselves so much that we burn out and become callous and ungiving. We need to know our limits with caring and giving. We need to know when it is time to pull back a little bit or take time for a rest. We are no good to others when we are burned out ourselves. It is important that we remain caring individuals, but too much caring can sometimes result in clinical depression or somatic illnesses, such as headaches, irritable bowel syndrome, or high blood pressure.

Too much caring can also result in relationship problems. There can be resentment and anger. That is why it is so important to know your own boundaries in life with regards to giving of your time and money. Most all of us want to be known as caring, giving individuals, and that remains an important aspect in living a content and fruitful life.

However, giving too much of ourselves, working too much, or giving too much of our money to others can sometimes rob us of needed peace and happiness and joy. In summary, there are a lot of beneficial aspects in caring. Neurotransmitters and hormones (serotonin, dopamine, and oxytocin) can be altered as a result of initiating the act of giving or caring. Changes in these hormones and neurotransmitters can alter our behavior. For some, there is more of a spiritual aspect of giving that ties into our perception of God and his generosity to humanity.

Caring for others can be one of the most rewarding things that we do in our lives. We do not have to be a doctor or a minister to care for others. We can care for others in any situation that we are in. Do not harden your heart so that you do not care about others, but also be sure to know your own limits.

WSC

Breathe:
Your Spiritual Oasis

In a life of many adventures, one experience continues to be my favorite.

I grew up around water. The Great Lakes region is my home. From infancy, the Fairley boys spent our summers at the family cottage on Mary Lake in Muskoka, Ontario. We took swimming lessons and enjoyed swimming at the Massey high school pool. Summers also included time at Forest Cliff Camp on Lake Huron. Later we had a pool in the backyard. Water, water, water. Swim, swam, swum.

It was not until my late 20s when visiting Grand Cayman that I had a transcendent experience in the water. One of the local dive shops was offering scuba diving for beginners. It was something I had always wanted to do, but it was not practical in the darker lakes of Canada's cottage country. The Cayman Islands are known as one of the best places to dive with their abundant coral reefs, crystal clear water, and white sandy shores.

The program began with a "resort course" in the hotel swimming pool. There, we learned the basics of the diving experience: the signals, rules, and what to expect it to be like. The next stage was to don the flippers and mask. Finally, the diving tanks were added.

To scuba dive, you put the regulator in your mouth and breathe in and out. Sounds simple, right? It is—and it isn't. For our entire lifetime, we have always breathed through our noses and mouths. This involuntary function is a matter of life and death. Now, a large device that is attached to a hose that is then attached to the air tank is how you will fill your lungs. Some people, even those who were comfortable swimming, just could not do it. Others found it to be no problem. What was the difference? Belief.

There was nothing complex about using the scuba tanks to breathe. All you had to do was relax, breathe in and out, and all would be well. But, you had to believe that this would work. If you could not trust, your fear would cause you to panic. In the swimming pool, that would be no problem. You would lift your head out of the water and breathe. If you are 50 feet underwater, it is a big problem.

Spirituality is a very broad area of life. It can include faith and religion, but it is more than just those. The sense of wonder we experience in looking at the stars, being enchanted by a piece of music, delighting in the beauty of a walk in the forest, enjoying a piece of art, reading a great story, or even learning about science can all touch us spiritually. Something transcendent happens that is more than just a function of our minds, emotions, or bodies. Poets, philosophers, theologians, writers, and artists have all tried to probe and understand what it is. It is the occupation of much of the area of education we call the humanities.

While it can be a collective experience, like a concert or religious service, in our time, spirituality is often very personal. What enchants us can be many things, or it might be more narrowly defined. It can change over our lifetime or have strands that follow us throughout all of our days.

In addition to the notion of something enchanting, words like "awakening" and "stirring" are often used to describe those first experiences when you begin to explore your spiritual self. Some people begin this engagement early in life, others in later years. Others never make much of a connection to that part of life.

What has your spiritual practice or experience been? Perhaps, you find solace in the rituals and spiritual disciplines of a faith. Are you nurtured by reading? Does music carry you to a quieter place for contemplation and reflection? How does your connection with your spirituality add to your sense of purpose or calling, as one who helps others? To what extent is your sense of service rooted in your spiritual experiences or in your awareness of life being more than just what we can touch?

There are many ways to explore the beauty of the Caribbean Sea that surrounds the Cayman Islands. You can see it in a video. You can stand on the beach and enjoy its amazing sights. You can snorkel over the shallow water and see some of the ocean life. A glass-bottom boat allows you to view some of the fish who happen by, or who are enjoying being fed by one of the tour guides. You can even board a submarine that will take you to the coral reefs below, along with a tour of the edge of the abyss at the end of the island shelf.

But if you really want to fully experience being in the moment with the life on the reef, you have to put on the scuba gear and descend into the depths.

Much of engaging the spiritual dimension of our lives rests on that same issue of trust, belief, or faith that I needed to scuba dive. If I was going to experience being actually present with the creatures, colors, and wonders of that coral reef, I would have to have faith.

Holding my mask on, I fell backwards into the water. Together, we began our slow descent. I had to remind myself, *Breathe in. Breathe out. Slow, deep breaths. In and out.* I now recognized that I was making the sounds of *Star Wars*. It was Darth Vader breathing. *Relax*, I told myself. *You can breathe.* Before long, I was enchanted by the ocean life all around me and stopped thinking about breathing. All was well.

We paused along the rope line at each of the 10 foot markers to allow our bodies to adjust to the changes in pressure created by our changing depth.

My faith was rewarded as our group of divers arrived fifty feet below the surface. The colors, textures, and strangeness of swimming there over the reef felt like I had entered a different existence. Looking up, I could see the surface that looked like a clear but moving roof. Reality had been turned upside down. As I exhaled, I saw the collection of my bubbles rise higher and higher, until they were out of sight.

Through the use of an adjustable weight belt and the compressed air of the scuba tanks, your body's buoyancy is neutralized. You neither rise nor sink. Your only movement is whatever your slowly moving flippers and the current might create. You have a strange sense of weightlessness that adds to the sense of being in not outer space, but ocean space. It was at once peaceful and exhilarating. I had a sense of being somewhere totally "other." None of it could have happened without my desire to explore this strange world within our world. I also had to have faith that I could breathe there, fifty feet below the surface.

If you are someone who includes your spirituality in your celebration of life, be sure to take time to continue to explore that. When the stresses of work and home build, journey again into the spiritual realm through prayer, meditation, fellowship, music, art, reading, or nature. Wherever your spiritual self is fed and nurtured, go to that place.

Your spiritual oasis awaits.

Take a deep breath.

GDF

Recreating Yourself

Burnout can be combatted by renewing your spirituality, as well as renewing yourself mentally and emotionally. The issue is that sometimes we reach dead ends or challenges that we have a difficult time facing or getting by, and we need to recreate our inner selves in order to move forward. Renewal of our spirituality might include a concerted effort for us to attend church more frequently or perhaps to read more spiritually-oriented books or to pray more. Renewing yourself spiritually might include going on a retreat, getting away from your surroundings for a while, and looking at yourself to see what needs changing. Renewing of our spirituality definitely must include resting. We have to take time to physically rest our bodies, as well as to rest our minds. By renewing ourselves spiritually, other parts of our lives tend to fall into place the way they are supposed to. If we are struggling to find spiritual renewal, perhaps we need to talk to one of our pastors or ministers or even a close friend that we trust who has been a source of spiritual guidance for us over the years.

How do we recreate ourselves emotionally? One of the ways that we can do this is through counseling or therapy. Talking to a therapist can be essential in helping us recharge our batteries and perhaps change our emotions. If our emotions are such that we need some medical assistance in stabilizing them, by all means we should pursue that. Perhaps we need antidepressants or medications for severe anxiety or other types of mood swings or emotional issues. We might find it difficult to recreate ourselves without assistance from others. Seek out a trustworthy individual to help, whether a friend, a trained professional, or a member of the clergy.

As we become weary in caregiving, sometimes our emotions reach a point of severe depression or anxiety. Trying to help with an elderly parent or perhaps run a busy clinical practice inevitably creates wear and tear over the years, and it is very important to take care of yourself emotionally and mentally. Sometimes we might have an innate desire to recreate ourselves when we discover that there are parts of our lives we do not like and that need to change. Perhaps a caring friend has pointed out an area of our lives that we can improve in, so that we can be in a better position to be compassionate towards others.

Perhaps we are working too hard and getting burned out. Or perhaps, as the title of this book suggests, we need to focus on finding our oasis. We need to find that thing or activity or group of people that help us refresh ourselves, that help us recreate ourselves. Again, this might include setting boundaries with those that are a drain on our spirits or our emotions. We might have to establish new friendships or modify the friendships that we already have, in order to recreate ourselves. If we do these things, then we can renew ourselves spiritually, mentally, and emotionally.

WSC

Into the Darkness

The helping professions, by definition, involve caring for those in need. Those needs might be physical, social, emotional, spiritual, mental, legal, or some combination of these.

Some of these needs are part of a chronic condition. The certified nursing assistant/personal support worker cares for the elderly patient. The counselor is there to hear and support the person mired in their challenges.

There are caregivers who serve those in a time of crisis. The minister comforts a family when there is a divorce or tragedy. The social worker intervenes when children are at risk. The first responders rush to a car accident. The lawyers and judges work on a case that includes unspeakable horrors. The teacher listens to a child describe a desperate home life. The hospice nurse helps a family say good-bye to their loved one. The undertaker is called to care for the body of a child who has died.

These intense experiences require caregivers who have not only compassion but courage as well. The intensity of the days, hours, or moments challenge each one to their core. The most human of tragedies, the most painful of experiences, the most unexpected moments in the life of the patient, client, parishioner, or the family member can cut deeply to your soul. You are present in their despair, rage, disbelief, and trauma. You not only are aware of the pain, but you are part of their story at some of the worst moments imaginable.

How do you process what you have witnessed? What are the choices beyond emotional neuropathy where nothing is felt again? In walling off these painful scenes, do you risk becoming desensitized to the beauty and wonder in the rest of your life? It is little wonder why so many relationships are destroyed when one of the partners is called to witness so much suffering. When you know so much about the horrors of life, how can you avoid the sanctuary of too many drinks, prescription meds, cigarettes, or other insulators from the human condition at its worst?

As a society, we do not begin to understand the cost we exact from so many of those people who are willing to care in the most extreme moments of life. These intense experiences, repeated over and over in a career of caring, cause burnout and deflection that can change you as a person. You know too much. You have seen too much. You have heard too much. You have felt too much.

Like trying to un-ring a bell that has sounded, the caregivers will not be able to return to the moment before they were called to be there for the crisis. It will always be different now.

Where is the hope for those we ask to serve on the front lines of horror? How do we begin to recognize the sacrifice that these professionals make on behalf of the individuals they help and society as a whole?

When your life regularly includes seeing people at their worst or most desperate, you increase your risks in so many important areas of your life. What can you do to avoid being cynical, numb, or angry at the expectations that your caregiving assumes?

As with anything in life, when we enter a place of heightened risk, we must take more precautions. If you are going on a boat, you increase your risk of drowning, so wear a life jacket. Buckle up when you are in a car. Use mitts before pulling hot food from the oven. Have a fire extinguisher in your kitchen. We do all of these things to minimize our risk and to have a solution if the worst happens.

In the caring professions, too often there is an assumption that whatever you will experience, it comes with the territory. You are expected to be ready for it and then handle it. Move on to what is ahead. Do not dwell on what has happened. Put it out of your mind.

Thankfully, many organizations do provide support for those who are on the frontline of disaster. Counseling, support groups, and time off are offered to those who have seen too much. But even in many of these supportive contexts, there is an assumption that you will ask for help if you need it. When you have been present at a horrible moment, your need to process it may not be recognized for a long time.

It is not unlike a concussion. You may be tackled in a football game or knocked into the boards of a hockey rink. You bang your head. You are stunned, but it seems that you are well enough to continue in the game. Only later do you begin to experience the effects of the concussion that you experienced. You may not have recognized your injury or the new risks of continuing to play with a concussion.

Caregivers serving those in critical moments can also be concussed by their experiences. The concussion may not be physical but could be emotional, spiritual, social, or mental. Instead of your brain being shaken, as happens with a physical concussion, your being may be shaken. The symptoms may follow later. The damage can be as intense and long-lasting as anything a collision of helmets might cause.

It is difficult for caregivers to advocate for themselves. As people who are focused on others, they tend to minimize their own challenges. After all, others are much worse off. The limited resources need to be spent on those with the greatest need. Their sense of calling and willingness to sacrifice themselves for others make it less likely that they will reach out for help or admit that they, too, need care. Even when they can mentally assent to the proposition that we need to care for our caregivers to sustain them in their service, they often never quite get around to making that call or sending that e-mail asking for support. Just as physicians and nurses make some of the worst patients, caregivers often prefer not to be on the receiving end of care. In some cases, they falsely believe that it will reflect negatively on their professionalism, if they ask for help.

Institutionally, we need to be proactive to monitor and care for these "wounded healers," as the Dutch priest and author Henri Nouwen so helpfully called them. This includes having regular check-ups. When there is an especially difficult, tragic, or intense experience, we need to insist that these frontline caregivers take time to talk, rest, and be supported. That's not easy to do, as these professionals can be very persuasive that they are ready to get back onto the field. There are always too few of them available, so it is tempting for leaders to accept their word that they are fine.

If we hope to maintain the quality and resilience of these professionals for the long-term, we must care enough to protect and support them, their families, and their careers. As a society, we can not afford to do anything less.

Inspiration

As I was preparing this chapter on inspiration, I thought about the basic definitions of *inspiring* and/or *inspiration*. It literally means "to breathe in air" or "to inhale." It can mean to fill someone with the urge or ability to do or feel something, especially something creative or passionate. Some of the synonyms that go along with *inspiration* include *motivation, encouragement, stimulation,* and *energy*. Where do we find inspiration for our lives? What inspires us? What motivates and energizes us? What galvanizes us?

I think there are several main areas in life from which people receive inspiration. The two main areas are being influenced by other people that we admire and, in a more spiritual realm, receiving inspiration from God. What breathes life into us? What is our motivation? Since this book is focused on caregivers and caregiving, we need to understand what motivates us to be caregivers. I think that when we find our oasis, when we discover that area of refreshment in our lives, then we can inspire both ourselves and others.

People we admire provide inspiration in our lives. On the other hand, when we see people that we do not necessarily like, we might be inspired to go in the direction opposite of the way their lives are going. Finding our inspiration from other people is important. We may be inspired by a family member to go into a certain profession. We might be inspired by a teacher who encouraged us to pursue a certain path in our lives. We might be inspired by a coach or personal trainer to exceed in the physical aspects of our lives. Perhaps a member of our clergy provides inspiration for us to pursue the spiritual aspects of our lives. It is important to identify what inspires us so that when we need inspiration, we will know avenues to get it.

Again, a lot of our inspiration comes from our mentors, parents, teachers, pastors, and role models. We might find inspiration through working with a therapist to help sort out some of the conflicts in our lives. Inspiration can also come from finding our oasis in life. It is important to understand what makes you tick, what excites you and motivates you. Identify those areas that inspire your heart. Pursue them.

As far as the spiritual aspect of life, it would be difficult for me to write a chapter on inspiration and not talk about God. There are spiritual connections with inspiration that motivate us to do good deeds to help others.

We might have been helped by someone else who inspired us, and therefore through its ripple effect, we help other people. We may have had some tragedy early in life and later ran across someone who experienced a similar tragedy; our shared story might enable us to inspire them in difficult times. Inspiration can even arise out of periods of depression and despair. Many times, those are the times in our lives when we look back and can identify someone or something that helped galvanize/inspire us for change.

First, we need to identify what inspires us and then we need to pursue it with passion. Without inspiration, there is little hope. Without inspiration, it will be hard to find your oasis. Without inspiration, there is no hope for weary caregivers. Whatever it takes, find your inspiration in your life.

WSC

One Life at a Time

Depending on the number of people you care for in a day or week, you may struggle with the tension of the one and the many.

When your role includes seeing many people, it can seem overwhelming at times. You are with a patient or client, but you are conscious of the five, ten, or twenty others who will also see you that day. As soon as you see your schedule, you realize that it will be busy—and that means many appointments.

Add to that the pressure of using "counseling minutes" wisely. How much can you cover in the time allocated for the meeting? Will you be able to review everything the client or patient is hoping to discuss? What questions need to be asked? How do you leave time for the silent moments that allow the person to gather his emotions or thoughts? Will you be able to allow the reflection that he needs to let your conversation take root?

If you are a physician, how much vital information can the patient convey for you to be able to make a diagnosis and recommend treatment? What needs to be said to the patient for him to be properly educated on the topic? If there are choices to be made, how do you maximize the time while still allowing the patient to consider the options? What will you do with your "doctor minutes"?

Educators are presented with the sea of faces that make up their class. Together, they are "the class." The class needs to cover a range of information from the curriculum to ensure that they have the benefit of the knowledge they will need for future classes—and ultimately for life and work. Yet, within that group, you have a wide range of language capabilities, study skills, learning channels, emotional maturity, and academic preparation. If your commitment also includes differentiated instruction, you must see "the class" as a collection of individual learners who benefit from exploring in ways and at a level appropriate to them as individuals.

For first responders, your work is a series of encounters with one or more individuals at a time. Each member of the public whom you serve will have his or her own crisis that will be unique, in spite of how many times you have been on a similar call. All of the variables of time, place, urgency, and specifics will shape the routines you apply to give the best of care. After you leave the scene or drop off the patient, you may have paperwork to complete, or it may be another call that takes you out again.

While we try to compartmentalize what happened yesterday, what happened already today, and what might happen later, our experiences do cross over. We can find ourselves thinking about that other event or challenge, even while we are meeting with our patient or client of the moment. Teachers who are talking with one student must still have their eyes and ears attuned to what else is going on in the room.

When we realize that our attention has drifted off the person of the moment in front of us, we feel frustrated with ourselves. That can lead to disappointment with our workplace for the volume of clients we must see in a day. It can even cause us to resent the student, patient, or client, since we can not care for the many while we focus on the needs of the one.

All of this can add to our compassion fatigue.

So many needs. So many demands. So little time.

What can be done?

How can you become "realistic" about the challenges? How do you avoid becoming seared and cynical toward those you are serving, which is another form of burnout?

Begin by acknowledging the obvious. There is only one of you and many of them. Most in the caring professions will serve in an under-staffed and under-resourced workplace. There will never be enough time to do all that can be done.

While this reality impacts you and those you serve directly, it is nothing personal! Many policy, resource, financial, and political consid-erations create the setting for your everyday experience. Couple that with the fact that we are dealing with human beings as leaders, facili-tators, managers, and support team members, and we must accept the reality that perfection will always be a long way off.

Take a pause. If possible, take a moment to reset your mind and attention. Close out the last file. Be conscious that you are beginning something new with a different person.

Personalize the moment. Make a point of using the client, patient, or student's name throughout the meeting. The mention of a name tells the person that you are paying attention to him as a person. It also reminds you that, as much as you have seen the challenges this person is facing before, this experience is unique for him.

Make eye contact. Being intentional about looking at someone is a quick reminder that the person you are serving is unique.

Be open to learn. Whenever we approach our time as an opportu-nity to learn, it changes us. We are more likely to actively listen, if we believe we might learn something.

See yourself in a story. Each of your moments in life when combined together becomes your life story. Many people see their work as a job to earn a paycheck. If you instead see your moment with the patient, client, or student as something in a book, movie, video game, or play, the moments take on a new importance. What is happening? What does it mean? How is it developing the story? Using a third-person perspective can enhance our ability to concentrate on the moment and the person we are serving at that time.

Prepare for an imaginary pop quiz. What if someone were to ask you about what happened in the appointment? How much could you remember? How many details did you notice? We have all had the experience of driving our usual route home at the end of the day. We remember leaving work. We know that we are now home. But we have no real memory of the trip we just traveled. If we believe that our memory of the experience is important, we tend to live in the moment more.

Most caregivers will always have the tension of the one and the many in their work. There are times to step back and see the big picture. But if we can choose each day, each appointment, to concentrate on the individual we are serving, we will find greater satisfaction with the important work that we do.

GDF

Colleagues in Crisis

For those who work in professional jobs that involve helping people, it is so important that we are available to help our colleagues in crisis. Many of us are compassionate and try to do the right thing, but sometimes this might lead to some type of emotional crisis. Crises can evolve as a result of family conflicts, medical illness, or financial situations. What do we do when a colleague is in crisis? It varies based on the level of the crisis and the specific care needs of the individual.

Many of us lead busy lives, and we do not pick up on the needs of others as well as we should. Many times colleagues might call us for help or perhaps to talk about a situation. If you are a physician, it is possible that a colleague might ask you to see them personally as a patient. So, what do we do? How do we help them?

Depending on our areas of expertise, the help and evaluation for a colleague in crisis might vary. First, it is important to listen. Take time out of your busy schedule to show empathy and caring for the colleague that has reached out for help. Sometimes, the colleagues themselves are not reaching out, but their families are encouraging them to seek support or perhaps the Board of Nursing or the Medical Board is requiring the colleague to reach out for help.

In these situations, we need to determine if our capacities and capabilities are enough to be able to help our colleagues or if they need a referral to a different individual who can better assist them. We need to clearly know our boundaries with regards to our abilities to help. If we personally do not have the time or resources to help, we should try to refer our colleagues to another healthcare provider—perhaps a minister, perhaps a financial adviser, depending on what the need is. We are not going to be able to help everyone.

We have limits to our own energy and time. We have limits based on financial obligations. Despite our limitations, there are quite a few options available to help colleagues who are in crisis. Again, the first step is simply to listen and identify what the crisis is. The fact that someone took the time to listen to them and care about them will make a world of difference; it is perhaps one of the most important things you can do in helping a colleague. It is not necessarily what is said or not said, but the fact that someone took time and listened, that someone took time and cared.

For more complex matters, we should do our best to get our colleagues to seek professional help. This might be some type of mental health professional if the problems revolve around mood disorders or substance abuse, or a different type of healthcare provider if the problems centers around physical illness. In each case, we must first find out what is causing the crisis. It might involve a relationship conflict. It might involve a problem paying the bills. Perhaps someone in the family has lost his job. Perhaps your colleague has lost his job. There are so many scenarios and ways that crises can occur and ways to resolve the crisis. So it is important that we avail ourselves to help our colleagues.

As we strive to help, we must practice self-awareness. We must know what we are able to do and what we are not able to do. If we are not able to meet the needs of a colleague in crisis, then we should get that colleague to someone else or some group or some other resource to help them in their crisis. If there are substance abuse issues going on, perhaps a referral to Alcoholics Anonymous or a drug rehab center is the appropriate care. Perhaps it means taking time out of our busy schedules to go over and visit a friend who is struggling, meet him for coffee or for a meal to support him and show that we care about him.

No matter what profession you are in, you are going to run into colleagues in crisis at some point in time. Be available to listen, take time, and care. It is also important to set boundaries for yourself so that you personally do not end up with compassion fatigue.

When Enough Is Enough

In a book that focuses on compassion fatigue, it would be incomplete not to have a chapter on when enough is enough. As caregivers, many times we will not even entertain the thought that we can walk away from giving and giving and giving. But sometimes that is exactly what needs to happen. Being unable to walk away from a situation can result in compassion fatigue. This book talks about boundaries with others and boundaries with ourselves. But this chapter focuses on the difficult topic of when enough is enough.

Many of us have been in situations where we give and give, and yet the situations do not appear to be changing. Some of us are working with clients or patients or family members or friends. We have given and given as much as we can, and we reach a point where the giving is actually hurting us. When we have crossed the line between helping others and hurting ourselves, that is the time to consider the fact that enough is enough. That is the time to consider walking away. We all want to help other people. We all want to fix the problem. But sometimes, fixing or solving is not within our capacity. Sometimes we have given of ourselves, given of our time, or perhaps even given financially, over and over again, and yet the people receiving these gifts are not using them to the best of their ability.

This is when the fact of tough love comes in. For example, imagine working with someone who is addicted to drugs or alcohol. Perhaps you have counseled them or talked to them or given them money to help out in a rough time. Perhaps they have said they are going to stop drinking or stop using drugs, but in fact, they have not stopped. Perhaps you have forgiven them and you have given more money, more time, or more effort. But they have continued to drink or steal or engage in some other type of unacceptable behavior. That is the time to ask yourself, "Is enough, enough? Is it time to walk away?"

I think that there are certainly times when enough is enough. I see this frequently, working with families, friends, or patients. We all have enabled others at some point in time. Sometimes giving and giving and giving to someone is not the right answer. Sometimes lending money for an "emergency" time after time after time is not the right answer. It is those times we have to question ourselves and look for guidance from others or God to set the boundary.

Setting boundaries and admitting enough is enough can actually help the other person. You may not notice the benefits immediately, but perhaps down the road, that person might come up to you and say, "Thanks. . . . Thanks for not enabling me. . . . Thanks for not giving money for my addiction." Sometimes, enough is enough, and we need to know what that is for us personally.

We all have limits with our physical abilities and emotional capacities. None of us is able to provide unlimited care or concern or finances for another person. We would like to think we could. We would like to think that we could always be that person to help when the phone rings or when we receive a request in a letter or an e-mail. We would like to think that we are superhumans who can rise above our limitations.

The fact of the matter is that all of us have limits based on what we can do for others. We all have limits, and there is nothing wrong with that. I think that our society promotes the concept of limitless giving, either financially, emotionally, or physically. Many of us are conditioned to be more giving than others. Some of us find it is easier to set boundaries than others. When we are dealing with a situation that consistently drains us, whether it is at work or in our personal lives, we need to decide for ourselves when enough is enough.

In dealing with relationships, there are going to be times when you want to try to change the other person or finance the other person, but instead you must act on what is right and walk away. There are those times when it is okay to set the boundary, when it is okay to walk away.

All of us need to find our oasis in life. Again, that oasis may be different for each individual. But once you have found that oasis, do not let it go. Do not let another person or situation rob you of your needed oasis. It is okay to give. It is okay to help others. But do not be afraid of walking away when enough is enough for you.

You do not have to feel guilty when you have done the best you can do and the situation did not change or the person did not change. We all want others to behave the way we want them to, but life usually doesn't work out that way. Walk away when it is time, and feel good about doing that.

WSC

Make Your Prison Break

Forgiving someone else does not change the person you forgive—it changes you.

The power to forgive is a great gift we have all been given but seldom use. Many do not realize that they have this essential ingredient for keeping relationships healthy. For those in the caring professions, it is vital that you understand and practice these principles.

The damage to relationships caused by the stresses and strains of life, combined with our many careless moments, leave us all with many scars. From our most casual encounters to our most intimate relationships, we find many ways to let down and hurt those we hardly know, those we love dearly, and those who are somewhere in between. This means we all have large and small offenses, both real and imagined, that consume our thoughts and emotions. Friends, family members, spouses, employers, colleagues, neighbors, and strangers can offend us at any moment. Sooner or later (usually sooner), someone will cross our boundary.

Even those of us not gifted in accounting or organization have an amazing ability to calculate and file away all of these offenses committed against us. We will even count those actions that were not done that we think should have been. Sins of commission and omission are all fair game.

Like a high-speed computer, we can access these files at a moment's notice with all the gory details included, like a paparazzi account where nothing is left out. As soon as we hear the person's name or see their face, it is all right there. Our muscles tighten and our fists clench at the thought of those who have wronged us again and again. Before long, we start to resemble the bitter old people we used to notice with curiosity when we were children.

The good news is that bitterness is not inevitable. There is a cure for our anger and hurt. The answer is in the power to forgive, something that we all have been given. It is the power to be free from the chains of painful and damaged relationships.

One of the common misconceptions when we talk about forgiveness is that it is better not to forgive: "That person does not deserve to be forgiven" or "What they did to me was so painful or hurts so much that I don't want to forgive them. I refuse." That misses the point of the gift we have received with forgiveness.

Forgiveness is primarily for the benefit of the person doing the forgiving.

Yes, there are certainly some benefits for someone who has been forgiven, and that is important too. But the first and principal benefit comes to the person who is willing to forgive. That's why we call it the power to forgive: When you choose to forgive, you are actually exercising your power in that relationship to move it forward and to take away the chains that very quickly surround a broken relationship.

Now, to be clear, forgiveness is not the same as justice. So, we are not talking here about crimes. This is not about something in the workplace or community that's inappropriate, illegal, or against company policy. Those justice or legal issues have to be dealt with appropriately through the proper authorities. This is not hiding the facts if there is something going on that is wrong or illegal. We are not talking about that at all. If a crime was committed, the authorities need to be notified. If it is something that violates company policy, that needs to be dealt with through the proper human resource channels or other authorities.

Forgiveness is about how we process our feelings on the personal side. If you take time to investigate an old hurt, you often discover that the person who hurt you does not remember, never knew, or does not care about all the churning and turmoil created in your life. Now, that may be the case for a number of reasons. It could be because they did not intend to do anything to hurt you. Perhaps it was neglect, or maybe it was a lack of sensitivity. Often, they do not have any memory of it because it wasn't something that ever appeared on their radar.

For the person who has accumulated this long list of grievances, it may come as a great shock to find the wrongdoer is unaware of his crimes. The victim has spent plenty of time going over and over this person's faults. The injured party, who did nothing to offend or provoke him, is bitter and upset. Yet, the guilty party may not even remember the vexing experience.

All that energy is being spent on someone who was ignorant of the offense or who does not care about having a positive relationship. The potential joy and good of that relationship is lost over something they never knew. That is a tragedy.

Of course, there are hurts that are very legitimate, where someone purposefully did something to undermine the relationship in order to hurt us. They might have worked to sabotage something in our lives, or they may have done something truly terrible. We must not minimize those kinds of actions, as they can be very real with lasting scars. Yet even with the most intentional hurts against us, it is still in our best interest to forgive that other person. Without forgiveness, that person will always have a negative link to us.

We cut that negative connection by saying, "I am choosing to forgive that person."

Remember, forgiveness does not deny your pain or claim that what happened did not happen. It does not assume that those who hurt you deserved forgiveness, asked to be forgiven, or are available to ask. (Perhaps they moved away or even died.) But you can still decide to forgive for your own well-being. Forgiveness begins by making a decision—not because you feel like doing it.

You choose to forgive to set yourself free.

If someone has offended you, it might be helpful to share that with him. This of course depends on the nature of the relationship. Someone you will never expect to see again is probably not a good candidate for this discussion.

However, if it is a colleague, family member, or friend, it might be worth the effort to let the person know how you are feeling. Done well and taken well, it can strengthen a relationship and avoid further conflict arising from careless behavior.

This should not be done as an ambush. It is best if it can be done in a neutral, casual setting like a coffee shop over a cup of coffee or iced tea. The point of going beyond your choice to forgive is to rebuild the relationship.

This needs to be shared carefully and with a humble approach.

Ask if the person would be willing to meet to discuss something that has been bothering you that you want to put behind you.

If you have such a relationship that they are willing to meet with you, think about what and how you are going to share your feelings. You might say, "I don't know if you are aware of this, but the other day when you said this (or you did that), it really hurt me. I really felt awful about that, and it's been bothering me. I just wanted to talk to you to see if we can work that out." Hopefully, that other person will say, "Wow, I had no idea. I didn't know there was something between us to talk about, sort out, or apologize for. Will you forgive me?" Then, you can move on with that relationship.

Forgiving others is good for them and best for us.

That's really the ideal, if possible. It doesn't always work that way, though. Sometimes, the other person is not available or willing to do that. He may wonder what all the fuss is about and just say that he did nothing wrong.

Remember, you can still choose to forgive these people, even if they do not ask to be forgiven or are unwilling to meet. Do not be surprised if they use the occasion to bring up something that may have been bothering them about you. Do not interpret that as getting even. It is probably a sense that since you are dealing with uncomfortable topics, you might as well get that out of the way too. If that happens, be prepared to apologize and ask for their forgiveness. Remember, like them, you may not have intended offense or even remember it either. A humble attitude is required for the sake of moving the relationship back on track.

Just as we receive our fair share of offenses, even the most careful people will offend their coworkers, friends, and family. You can always own up to your mistakes or missed opportunities by going to the person as soon as possible and acknowledging what happened. You will find most people are surprised that you would take the risk of doing that. They will respect the fact that you can not only recognize your mistakes but admit them too.

So many people lose their energy, robbed of their vitality and their sense of the joy of life by these bitter feelings. Even beyond forgiving, it is possible to forget, as well. That may sound impossible, and you may be tempted to say, "I will forgive, but I won't forget!" But that also keeps you from the more complete experience of moving past those things that hold you back. The next time you are reminded of what someone else did to offend you, practice forgiveness. Say, "Yes, I choose to forgive that person." Maybe you will see him across the table or at a meeting.

Say to yourself, "I choose to forgive." By that practice, you choose to move on, and that is very liberating. For that reason, we encourage you to just get into that practice of forgiving. If you get into the habit and practice of choosing to forgive, you will be surprised to find out that you really can also forget as well. That gives you the freedom to break the chains and move on to become your best self.

Choosing to forgive others is choosing to free our tomorrows.

GDF

Leading Caregivers

For those in a managerial role of guiding or leading caregivers, it is important to educate caregivers about their role of self-care. If caregivers are personally not taking care of themselves, they will be less effective in taking care of others. Self-care involves having enough personal time for yourself, getting plenty of rest, and exercising. Also self-care involves eating properly and not just bingeing on snack foods or junk foods. The most important challenge for supervisors, managers, and administrators of caregivers is to encourage self-care.

Those who lead caregivers must become educated regarding the signs of burnout. One of the key purposes of this book is to recognize what burnout is and how to prevent it. As a leader of caregivers, it is important to be available to counsel them individually or in a group regarding boundaries. It all comes down to boundaries. We can only do so much. That is not a defeatist attitude, but it is a realistic perspective on caregiving. As caregivers, we are also human beings, and we have to take care of ourselves, our families, and our jobs. Many of us are trying to juggle our schedules with the demands of our jobs and families, as well as taking care of a sick loved one. One of the ways that we can become more effective in leading caregivers is teaching them how to delegate responsibilities. One person cannot do all the caregiving for an individual. Therefore, delegation of responsibilities and boundaries is essential. Delegate the roles of the supervisors, managers, and administrators so that there will not be any duplication in job responsibilities.

Personal boundaries are where you end and another person begins. Boundaries regarding time and the ability to provide care are essential in helping us be the best caregivers we can be. Another way of supporting caregivers is to offer an educational retreat or a seminar about the roles of caregiving, boundaries, preventing burnout, and how to delegate responsibilities. Having an educational seminar like this will give the supervisors and managers a break from the daily routine and will also give them opportunity to interact with other individuals in supervisory or managerial roles. There can be a lot of benefits to exchanging ideas with those who are in those positions. As a supervisor, manager, administrator of caregivers, try to meet regularly with them, either individually or in a group. Because one of the major challenges of caregiving is burning out, it is essential to focus on ways to prevent burnout in your staff. Try to identify if any of your supervisors or managers are showing signs of burnout and take necessary steps to help them.

If what you are doing in respect to leading caregivers is not enough, and a supervisor or manager or administrator get burned out or clinically depressed or develops severe anxiety, it is imperative that you refer that individual for professional help. This might include counseling and/or medications. Perhaps they may need a break or a medical leave from work. Do not ignore the signs of burnout in your staff. Also encourage a healthy balance between caregiving and a personal life. Taking necessary breaks from caregiving (whether choosing medications or taking a timeout from work) is essential to sustain supervisors, managers, and administrators. They cannot work 24/7 month after month after month without a break.

For those who are leaders, or for those who are called to lead from time to time, I would recommend my friend Grant Fairley's book, *Positive Influence: How to Lead Your World*. (More information can be found in the Resources section at the end of this book.)

In summary, the opportunity to lead caregivers can bring great rewards, but it can also bring challenges. Be prepared for the challenges and be thankful for the rewards.

WSC

Choosing Your Battles

There is only so much of us to go around. No matter who we are or what we do, we only have 24 hours in a day. It does not matter if we are the president or if we are a teacher, a minister, or a physician. We all have to choose our battles wisely. What can we do best? Who can we help, and who should we help? That is the focus of this chapter.

To answer to these questions, we must first try to understand ourselves better, including both our strengths and our weaknesses. We need to understand how our life experiences or educations can give us guidance as to what we can do best when we help others. There are individuals who are perhaps in the ministry, but they find that they do better visiting the elderly in nursing homes or hospitals. Others find that they do best giving sermons. In the field of law, some attorneys do better in the courtroom, and others do better with real estate transactions. All of us have different talents that we need to identify and use to help others in the best way possible. After we have identified what we do best, whether it is in the area of teaching, counseling, comforting, or something else, we then need to identify who we can help.

Lots of times, we have idealistic views of who can we help. There is nothing wrong with that. I think one of the most important things to identify is that we can help those who are around us. Sometimes, we are led to go to the far ends of the Earth, including Africa or India or China, but most of us find that we are able to help those within our own families or in our office or in our jobs. Many times, we look to the future and say, "When I get to be a certain age, then I will help others." But we should be helping others no matter what age we are. We should help those who are already around us.

Again, sometimes we are led to go to the far regions of Africa, but there are people in need just in our own community, perhaps even a few miles from where we live or work. Identify with your talents and time those you can help. Sometimes, individuals do not want help or do not readily ask for help. Do not force your help on those who do not want it. That does not mean that we should limit our help to those who are just asking for it, because sometimes individuals need help and they are just reluctant to ask.

How do we know when we should help and when we should walk away? When is helping others hurting ourselves? What we try to do is to find a balance between helping ourselves and helping others. This goes back to the chapter on boundaries. We cannot be of much help to others if we are worn down and sickly ourselves. As the saying goes, you can't pour from an empty cup. We need to do what we can do to maintain our own health, physical and mental and spiritual, so that we will be able to reach out and help other people. There are those of us who would like to help lots of people, but we must contend with the realities of limited budgets, limited time, and for some, health issues.

When should you walk away? When you have done all that you can do to help someone or a group and you find that it is starting to wear on you too much, that is the time to do some self-reflection and see if it is time to walk away. There are times in our lives where we are working with other people on a community project or a church project, and it becomes too much of a strain to continue. Perhaps we had more time for a few months, but that time has run out. We need to learn to delegate or to refer responsibilities to others who have the needed energy or resources to help that person or complete that project.

We are not called to help and help and help to the point of physical and mental exhaustion. We are supposed to treat others as we would want to be treated. Would we want others to help us until they were broken down and worn out? Of course not. So again, when should we walk away? When working with others, sometimes they need a break from help. Sometimes help is episodic instead of continual. There are those who are unable to recognize their need for help and become quite hostile if you try to help them. There are others who will take as much help as you will offer, and they will never quite be satisfied. Sometimes we need to ask ourselves if it is better to help certain people at a later point in time or delegate the task to someone else who perhaps can do it better than you or who has more time or energy.

It is difficult to choose our battles. It is difficult to determine what we can do best to help other people and to identify who we can help. Remember that we can help those who are immediately around us first, as most of us are not called to go overseas to help those in need.

Who should we help? We should help those who have an identified need for which we are trained or educated. In the field of medicine, doctors help their patients. Different specialties/positions help those with problems in the particular area they are trained in. Attorneys help those who need guidance in the area of law they are trained in and have experience in. Teachers help those in the grade of school they are certified in or specifically trained in. Those who are led to provide supportive counseling do so for those who are in need, based on their level of comfort and education.

Choosing our battles can cause us to look at shades of gray. There are ethical considerations, religious considerations, and political considerations. It is important to help those who are unable to help themselves. Be sure to take care of yourself so that you can be a resource for others. There is hope for weary caregivers. We are not able to help everyone. But we are able to help some people. Choose your battles wisely.

WSC

Coping with the Age of Confusion

If we all live long enough, we will be dealing with either an elderly spouse or an elderly parent. Many times, as we age, medical illnesses such as dementia develop. It is such a saddening experience to watch your spouse or parent lose their memory, whether it happens slowly or quickly. Dementia is a very unforgiving illness. It can affect anyone, regardless of race, gender, or socioeconomic status. The struggles of taking care of an elderly spouse or parent can be immense. Without proper education and support, this can be quite a trial.

We never know if we will someday have to care for an elderly spouse who has special needs. But the best thing to do is to prepare for this possibility. Have those conversations earlier in life about what to do when you or your spouse might become disabled. Who will provide care? How will we pay the bills? What are our wishes regarding being resuscitated in the event of a cardiopulmonary event? Who do we want to have taking care of us, from a legal perspective, when we become not able to make financial or medical decisions for ourselves? Develop a plan of action sooner rather than later. Have conversations about what to do if your spouse becomes disabled or what to do if both of you become disabled at the same time. Do you have finances and support to do in-home care versus assisted-living care versus nursing home care? These are very tough questions that most of us tend to avoid because they are very painful to deal with.

When taking care of an elderly spouse with dementia or other medical problems, remember that we must take care of ourselves first. It is very altruistic and loving to care for your spouse or parents in the final stage of life; however, if you do not take care of yourself, you cannot be as effective in taking care of your loved ones. Also be careful that you do not lose your identity in taking care of your spouse or parent. Continue to take time to do some things that you enjoy. Reach out and spend time with friends. Do not let your friendships lapse because you have an aging spouse or parent who requires a lot of care. Not taking care of yourself will only lead to depression, anxiety, and despair. You might even become resentful and angry for having to handle the situation that has been dealt to you. To avoid burnout, it is essential to take breaks. Take some time to yourself so that you can rest and recharge your batteries. Then when you come back, you can continue the marathon of taking care of your loved one. You are not saying that you love your spouse or parent less, by taking a break. Remember, you're human. We all have physical and emotional limitations. We can only do so much. We have to be ready for the marathon, as end-of-life illnesses can sometimes last for years.

It is very important to identify and utilize your medical resources for treating the medical needs of your spouse or parent. Appropriate diagnosis and treatment will make your job easier. I am not saying easy, but easier. Utilize the resources of your pastor or priest or rabbi for spiritual support. Keep in contact with your friends and support system via the social media or the telephone. Many individuals set up Facebook pages so that their friends and family can keep up with the status of their loved one. There is not an easier way to dispense information in a short period of time. Many have found that this is quite a useful tool to assist them and their family and friends.

When taking care of an aging spouse or parent, the major challenge is to take care of yourself in the process. You, too, need rest. You, too, need social interaction. You, too, need breaks from providing care. Failure to take care of yourself will only lead to compassion fatigue. The purpose of this book is to help those caretakers, in whatever roles they are providing, to avoid compassion fatigue; if compassion fatigue develops, identify it and take care of it as soon as possible. A network of family, friends, and medical and emotional resources is the best way to combat compassion fatigue. Compassion fatigue is not 100 percent preventable when you are a caretaker. But if we educate ourselves and put the necessary support systems in place, we can have the best case scenario in taking care of ourselves and our loved ones.

WSC

Your Oasis of Hope

Mythology is meant to create a narrative around origins. If we look at any mythical story, it basically tells us why something is, where something came from, or what we are intended to do with it. In Greek mythology, Prometheus stole fire from the gods and gave it to humanity. This simple myth tells us the origin of how we discovered fire, and it is to Prometheus' credit that humanity strives to better itself in scientific and natural discovery. Zeus, however, was incredibly angry at Prometheus' transgression and delivered a particularly gruesome punishment upon him. Mighty Zeus blamed not just Prometheus for giving the gift, but he also faulted humanity for accepting this gift intended only for the gods. He had a penalty in mind for humanity, as well, in the form of a box and the beautiful woman who possessed it.

Zeus was very clear in his instructions. Pandora could have the container, but not its contents. She was never to open the box, and what it contained must be sealed within it forever. Beautiful Pandora must have sat daily, staring at the one thing she could not have. Fashioned by Zeus and gifted to Prometheus' brother, Pandora was created with an insatiable curiosity—a carefully crafted curiosity that would play perfectly into the nasty trick of vengeance he had planned.

Let's imagine the story playing out. Day after day, Pandora sits. The box never far from her sight, Pandora watches. She is consumed with the curiosity that courses through her, unable to focus on anything else for very long other than what the box holds. Finally, her impulses prove too strong to be mastered. She gives in, takes the box to a quiet place, and opens it. Paintings vividly depict the rushing out of all the world's evil as Pandora lifts the lid. Ugly and contorted wraiths fly from the box—released upon an ill-prepared and undeserving world. Thus evil and sin now lurk in the shadows of the living. Pandora, frightened and ashamed, slams shut the lid in fearful remorse, trapping the last of the box's contents, hope. Unable to escape or perhaps unconcerned, hope remains something humans can hold onto—something still in the box, something meant to mend the chaotic mélange of malice around us.

It is understood that everything in the box rushed out in a desire to be free, and therein lies the origin story. It's the myth of how evil entered the world, and how we still retain possession of hope, the one true gift that was in the box. Yet, how much do we question Zeus' intention? Why in the world would he have packed this particular present? Sure, it makes perfect sense to collect a selection of related items and wrap them up in a basket to give as a gift. We do it all the time. We simply get a basket or a box or a bag and fill it with a bottle of wine, a glass or two, perhaps a cork screw, and a couple of pieces of gourmet cheese. Voila! A perfect gift. But how curious would it be to add to that basket an unrelated item, say a crow bar or a pencil sharpener? It doesn't make sense. Neither, really, do the contents of Pandora's box: greed, envy, hatred, pain, disease, hunger, poverty, war, despair, death, etc. And then, thought Zeus, let's throw in hope just to confuse the issue.

Most of what Zeus gave Pandora and all of what Pandora unleashed unto the world is darkness. The funny thing about darkness is that it retreats from light. It flees from the light and is defeated by it. Strike a match or turn on a flashlight in a darkened room and notice what happens to the darkness—it seeks shelter from the light. It recedes and crouches in corners and beneath beds, behind doors, and under tables, where the monsters lurk.

Imagine, if you will, a capricious Zeus gleefully rummaging around in some cosmic compost of evil, digging out his select gifts, and placing them carefully in the box, knowing the way all the gods know that evil sits and festers and decays. In itself, it is unmoving. It is stagnant and rotten, but Zeus knows what he wants. He wants these unpleasant gifts to find their way into our world and rot us from the inside out, but he understands they won't move on their own accord, satisfied simply to decay in their own stench. So, he must create a hostile environment for the darkness, something that will propel it outward when Pandora unlatches the box, something from which it will flee. But what? Then he gets a flash of inspiration, a lightning bolt of an idea, if you will, and he reaches beyond the compost pile and into the sun, to pluck out a little bit of light that he calls hope. He drops it into the far right corner of the box and smiles in satisfaction as he watches what happens.

That little tiny bit of light illuminates the box and the darkness within it. The negativity, the greed, the hatred, the despair, and everything else he rooted from the trash to create his grab bag of doom retreats to the upper left corner of the box, searching for shadows that aren't there in which to hide. The darkness squirms and is so agitated that he raises a hand to divinely compel its stillness as it tries to slip over the edge to slither back to its cold and comfortable darkness.

Zeus knows he will have his revenge. He knows that Pandora's natural inclinations—inclinations he created for this purpose only—will push her until she can no longer resist. He also knows that his little gifts, so pent up and defeated, will have no choice but to rush out in fear and frustration to seek the dark corners of their new earthly home—the hearts of human beings. There is too much light in the box, and there is too much light in the world. Only in the hearts of human beings can evil lay dormant and rotting.

In all his presumed omnipotence, Zeus really didn't understand what hope would do to his plan. He didn't recognize that where hope exists, evil is already defeated. He didn't realize that what he intended merely as a catalyst for movement would actually add a counteractive balance to his nefarious plan.

What we often forget is that hope is always with us. Through our struggles, and despite our exhaustion from caring for our loved ones, or ministering to the needy, or helping others in our profession, we often forget to look for what defeats the darkness. We forget to look for light.

However we are called to do it, caring for other people is difficult. Caring for other people makes us vulnerable. Being vulnerable comes with a price, and though it is a price most of us are willing to pay, it nevertheless always seems that our debtors "come a-callin'" right when we have run out of resources. We just don't have the money to pay in full when the bill comes due, so we take out more credit than we have. We push ourselves too far. We borrow from our peace and our families, our hobbies and our joy, and as a result, there are times when we feel hopeless and exhausted, fatigued, angry, and frustrated—as if nothing has ever gone or ever will go right again. Our natural resources are depleted, and then our reserves begin to run perilously low, leaving us feeling too tired to peer through the darkness to look for the one thing that will defeat it.

Hope is a universal experience. It does not exist for any one group of people over another. One faith tradition doesn't have the market cornered, and there are examples of hope in all major world religions— even in belief systems that don't have a deity at their center. The Book of Lamentations in the Christian Bible offers a vital key in understanding how hope relates to whatever storms are swirling around and inside of us. In this collection of five lengthy poems, the speaker laments the harsh conditions of life, crying out in all his woes:

> *My soul is deprived of peace,*
> *I have forgotten what happiness is;*
> *I tell myself my future is lost,*
> *all that I hoped for from the Lord.*
> *The thought of my homeless poverty is wormwood and gall;*
> *Remembering it over and over*
> *leaves my soul downcast within me.*
> —Lamentations 3:17-20, NAB

This is exactly what we do when we are exhausted from caring, when we are prone to despair, and when hopelessness begins to creep in. We focus on the darkness. We roll around in our exhaustion. We tend the Devil's garden. But following this passage, near the actual center of the book in chapter 3 verse 21, the speaker gives us the key to understanding hope:

> *But I will call this to mind,*
> *as my reason to have hope:*
> *The favors of the Lord are not exhausted,*
> *his mercies are not spent.*
> —Lamentations 3:20-21, NAB

Hope is possible for us all. Even in the harshest of times, hope can exist and flourish, keeping us going, helping us move and breathe and live, giving us the tiniest extra bit of energy, understanding, and resolve that we need. But it does ask of us one thing.

We must acknowledge its existence. We must understand that it is there. We must seek its light no matter how piercing the darkness is. We must remember that evil fled from hope, and when we call this to mind, when we recall that good still exists, when we take a moment to look around for the light, we activate the hope that resides permanently within us. That is the one thing that hope asks of us. To acknowledge it. To use it. To call it to mind.

All of the suggestions that you have read in this book—the survival circle, venting your feelings to a trusted friend, discovering your oasis, making time to refresh yourself, understanding your inside world, and all of the rest, along with whatever individual little things you do to feed your own soul and care for yourself—these are the little lights of hope that carry a brightness from which evil, from which despair, from which exhaustion, from which every conceivable negative feeling flees.

Hope is with us. And if we can't see it, we simply must look for it. We must call it to mind; we must activate it. It's in everything we do. It's in how we deal with the most difficult clients; it's in our most enjoyable hobbies. It is why we do what we do. When we are caring for other people, we are not fixing them. We are not curing a disease or erasing a mental illness. We are helping those people exist as comfortably as they can. We are pointing out to them the light they have within themselves. We are showing them hope, even when they feel they can't see it. Why not try and do the same for ourselves?

Hope is not a fantasy. It is not a wish for better days or different circumstances. It is a very real thing—a very real thing that simply helps us survive in a particular situation. We can't always change our present moments. Sometimes, our loved ones are sick. Sometimes, we lose our jobs. Sometimes, we have unimaginable sorrow. Sometimes, we are exhausted and feel like we cannot do this for another day. But all the time, hope whispers that we can. Hope says indeed we can, and we must. Always burning within us, it flashes in those dark moments like a beacon, just enough to help us see it. We simply have to peer through darkness and focus on that spark. The beauty of it is this: simply by looking for it, by calling it to mind, by believing in the possibility of what hope has to offer, we are activating and strengthening it.

CLR

With

It was that time in the wedding ceremony for the minister to speak. Dr. Bruce Neal began his charge to the couple by saying a small word: "with." Like all gifted speakers, he was able to take those gathered on a journey that connected that word to life and relationships. I never forgot it. I should never forget it. I was the groom who was receiving the challenge to pay attention and be truly "with" my wife, Cari, in our future relationship.

"With" is the essence in the work of all who serve others. Nurses are with their patients. Teachers are with their students. Social workers are with their clients. Parents are with their special needs child. Emergency workers are with the sick and injured. Ministers are with a grieving family. Children are with their aging parent who needs more support. Community workers are with their hungry clients.

Being with is one of the greatest gifts that we can give to another human being who is in need. Caregivers may have many other solutions, supports, treatments, and programs to offer those in their care. As seasoned members of the helping professions will affirm, being present is essential.

Sometimes, being physically with the other person is enough. The presence of a police officer in a time of danger reassures those around him. There are times when sitting in silence with another person is the most helpful thing you can do.

When you are with someone in an emotionally difficult situation, the ability to listen and show empathy provides comfort, understanding, and support.

When you are the person in need, the absence of having someone with you is to be alone. The feeling of being alone in a time of need can make any experience much more difficult. No matter the pain or distress, the presence of another who chooses to be with us gives us courage to face the dark times.

The work of helping others is often a slow process where changes and results seem elusive and distant. It is easy to conclude that our efforts are futile because we do not see the outcomes we hoped would be apparent by now. Problems created over a lifetime are not easy challenges to solve. Life events can be so catastrophic that recovery will be slow and uncertain. It is easy to become discouraged.

The power of being with another person in need is already a gift to them. Your presence gives hope to the hopeless, comfort to the suffering, and courage to the discouraged.

When you think back to the difficult moments in your life, you may not be able to remember the treatment details or the words that were said. What you will remember is who was there with you.

While there are times when the help of one caregiver is sufficient, it is encouraging to know that others can be with you, if needed. Patients, clients, or members of the public who are in your care benefit from the collaboration and teamwork of your colleagues, associates, and coworkers. The greater the need, the more vital it is to have others with you, as you are with those in your care.

My parents each had an end-of-life journey that involved the support of our local hospice. Our community not only has support for patients in hospital and at home, it also has two hospice villages. There, patients receive excellent end-of-life medical care and support. The village also provides the opportunity to have family remain with their loved ones around the clock. In rooms that can be decorated with items from the patient's home, family members can be with each other and with those who come to visit.

Think of all of the people who will look back on some of the most painful, tragic, and challenging times of their lives. Their story and your legacy is that you were there with them at those profoundly difficult moments. You lent them hope. You treated their bodies, nurtured their minds, comforted their emotions, or inspired their spirits. You were with them.

Caregiving is choosing to be *with* those in need. Thank you for being that compassionate caregiver *with* the people in your story.

GDF

A Final Two Words

Our purpose in writing this book was to encourage you. We understand that caregiving is not an easy calling. It takes a special person to fill that role—to be someone who cares.

The needs around us can be overwhelming. There is so much pain, so much brokenness, so many people and families in distress. Fear, stress, and despair invade our lives, turning once-happy places into realms of sadness.

To those in the caring professions—the first responders, the educators, the healthcare teams, the civil servants, the daycare workers, the community support groups, the ministers, the elder care professionals, and so many more—let us say those magic words again. ***Thank you!***

Many days, you may serve and care for others without hearing those words. But rest assured, your work is always valuable.

Paychecks are necessary and appropriate for those who care for others. However, the true currency of the compassionate caregiver is the satisfaction that comes from helping others. The bonus is when someone recognizes your contribution and shares their appreciation for your diligent and kind service.

Your patients, clients, or charges may not be able to say thank you, due to their physical, emotional, or mental limitations. Some who are in an acute crisis are so focused on their own survival that gratitude doesn't occur to them until later on. There are times when your care might not be noticed or appreciated. There are also heroic moments when you make an immediate difference in someone's life. But often, it is somewhere in between. The slow, methodical, consistent, and persistent service you give is what is needed to improve someone else's quality of life.

We are better as a society knowing that our caregivers and their services exist. It may not occur to us every day, but there is a quiet comfort in knowing that your community is served by first responders, even if your loved ones have never needed an ambulance, even if your own house has never been on fire. When government functions well, we benefit from our ability to live our lives, do our jobs, and earn a living. When we know that those in crisis in our society will receive quality care, this benefits all members of the community. We all live with the awareness, at some level, that "it" could happen to us, too.

Whether it is your life's work or something you choose to do outside of your career, your service and caring is what binds the wounds of society. Continue to share hope with those who are in despair. Be the candle in the darkness.

Discover your oasis. Visit it often. Avoid burnout. Escape compassion fatigue. Share what you learn with the next generation.

On behalf of the many sick and suffering souls in our society who desperately need your care—and need you to take care of yourself—let us say our final two words:

Thank you!

BPH
CLR
GBL
GDF
LDK
WSC

About the Contributors

Brenda P. Hines, M.D.

Brenda Hines, MD, Associate Medical Director of
Somnus Sleep Clinic, Flowood, Mississippi

Dr. Brenda Hines grew up in Mississippi and continues to practice
medicine there. She graduated with a BS degree from Mississippi State
University and earned her MD from The University of Mississippi School
of Medicine. She trained in Pediatrics and Family Medicine at UMC and
practiced primary care from 1982 until 1992. She then returned to UMC
and trained in psychiatry. She has practiced in many different areas in
the field of psychiatry. While training in psychiatry, Dr. Hines developed

a special interest in sleep medicine. She is board certified in Psychiatry and Sleep Medicine and now limits her practice to sleep medicine. She lives in Mississippi, where she practices all aspects of sleep medicine in children and adults of all ages.

Lawrence D. Komer, MD, FRCSC

Dr. Lawrence D. Komer is the coauthor of the book *New Hope for Concussions, TBI, and PTSD*. This book describes his innovative research and treatment of people with head injuries from sports, military service, car accidents, workplace injuries, and everyday life. His coauthor and wife, Joan Chandler Komer, also share their personal journey with a loved one who was injured.

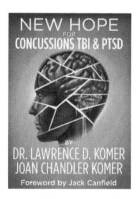

Dr. Komer is a sought-after expert and authority in restoring hormones, health, performance, happiness, and vitality. This new area of medicine is called Interventional Endocrinology. He has pioneered several treatment methods recognized as leading-edge protocols for the treatment of menopause, andropause (low testosterone), and traumatic brain injury.

Dr. Komer trained at Queen's University, Kingston, Ontario, earning a degree in physiology (the science of how living organisms function). He went on to receive his MD at Queen's and then went to McMaster University, Hamilton, Ontario, where he earned his specialty degree in Obstetrics and Gynecology. Dr. Komer is an Associate Clinical Professor at the Michael G. DeGroote School of Medicine, McMaster University, Hamilton, Ontario.

He joined the staff of the Joseph Brant Memorial Hospital in Burlington, Ontario, in 1976 and since then has delivered almost 13,000 babies. He introduced many new gynecologic techniques to the hospital, including operative endoscopic surgery, operative tubal surgery and reversal of sterilization, gynecologic laser surgery, and diagnostic and operative hysteroscopy. He also founded the Bone Health Clinic during his research in osteoporosis. His office practice has included a wide range of gynecologic assessments, but in the last twenty years he has focused on hormonal evaluation and hormone-replacement therapy (Interventional Endocrinology).

Dr. Komer has been a leader in the treatment of menopause, writing guidelines for physicians and delivering more than 100 talks entitled "Be Menopositive" with his wife Joan. He has assessed and successfully treated over 13,000 women suffering from poor hormonal function.

In 2004, he became Founder and Director of the Masters Men's Clinic. This is the largest clinic in Canada diagnosing, treating, and doing research on testosterone deficiency syndrome. The clinic has assessed and treated more than 6,000 patients.

Dr. Komer has been on the Board of Directors of the Canadian Society for the Study of the Aging Male. During that time, he observed the link between traumatic brain injury and low hormones in both men and women and has been a leading advocate for hormonal restoration to re-establish normal brain function.

In 2016, Dr. Komer was the recipient of the prestigious Physician Care Award.

Blair Lamb, MD, FCFP

Dr. Blair Lamb has practiced in the field of rehabilitative medicine for twenty-five years, using both non-interventional and interventional methods and modalities that facilitate the rehabilitation of most acute and chronic regional and global pain conditions. Dr. Lamb has multiple patents in spinal rehabilitation treatment, opiate side effect medication, opiate overuse medication, opiate withdrawal devices, trigger point dissolution medication, and shock wave treatment. He has created advanced specific treatment protocols for complex conditions, such FMS (fibromyalgia syndrome), post-concussion syndrome, TMJ (temporomandibular joint syndrome), RSI (repetitive strain injury), RSD (reflex sympathetic dystrophy syndrome), dystonia (Parkinson's), migraine headache, and more. Dr. Lamb is a graduate of the University of Western Ontario Medical School. His practice is in Burlington, Ontario, Canada.

www.drlamb.com
www.spinalsolutions.ca
@DrBlairLambMD

Chris L. Redden, LPC, NCC, CST

Chris is currently in private practice as a Licensed Professional Counselor in Baton Rouge, LA, with the Health and Counseling Center, LLC, as well as a school counselor in a Baton Rouge high school. He holds a BA in Philosophy and Religious Studies from St. Joseph Seminary College in St. Benedict, LA, and an MA in Theology from Notre Dame School of Theology in New Orleans, LA, as well as an M.Ed. in Counselor Education from Southeastern LA University in Hammond, LA. He also hold a certification as a sex therapist from the Modern Sex Institutes in West Palm Beach, Florida. He works with the Catholic Diocese of Baton Rouge educating children and adults about the prevention of sexual assault as a Child Protection Coordinator, and he educates high school students about sexuality, sexual consent, and modern relationship issues. In Chris' private practice, he sees clients facing a number of issues, but most of his work centers around the sometimes hostile intersection of faith and sexuality. His unique training and education affords him the knowledge and experience to help people navigate these two quite personal and important aspects of life. Chris hopes to continue exploring this dynamic into the next phase of his professional career and is grateful to the authors to be able to contribute to this book.

chris.redden@gmail.com
https://www.healthandcounselingcenter.com/

End Notes

The writers of this book see themselves less as authors and more as messengers who are passing along what they have received. We are indebted to many professors, teachers, mentors, authors, speakers, friends, and patients who have taught us about the topics considered in this book. There are too many sources to begin to credit—even if we could retrace where we first learned each underlying principle, concept, or perspective. Rather than to present an academic review of studies and data, the purpose here is to provide an accessible overview to allow readers to think about their journey. As such, we include some end notes to highlight places for readers to explore further on their own. If you recognize on an oversight on our part, please contact us at books@silverwoods-publishing.com so that we may update the book. We do not doubt that if we had the benefit of speaking with each of those who will read this book, we would have many additional ideas and perspectives to share.

The professional opinions of the contributors are their own. This book provides general information. Always consult your health and other professionals for advice on what is best for you.

Discover Your Oasis

Charles Frederick Williams led a fascinating life as a Victorian era war correspondent, editor, military commentator, and author. At heart, he was an adventurer and a storyteller who traveled to distant and troubled lands. The reports from the war correspondents provided much of the drama to be found in the news. Their coverage of the many campaigns of the British Empire and other conflicts were read around the world. Like the great explorers of their time, their exploits captured the imagination of readers in an age before radio, television, or digital media. In England, Charles Williams was at the center of political and social life during a time when Britain not only ruled the waves but also dominated the worlds of commerce and culture too. His life caught many of the most interesting currents of his era leading to friendships and shared experiences with many of the great, the good, and the colorful characters of his time.

One of our writers, Grant D. Fairley, is the great-great-grandson of war correspondent, Charles Williams.

Learn more about Charles Williams by visiting the Wikipedia page: https://en.wikipedia.org/wiki/Charles_Frederick_Williams

Discover Your Sleep Oasis

Here are a couple of books for those who would like to explore this topic in depth.

Kryger, Meir H., William C. Dement, and Thomas Roth. *Principles and Practice of Sleep Medicine*. 4th ed. Philadelphia: Elsevier Saunders, 2017.

Chokroverty, Sudhansu. *Sleep Disorders Medicine: Basic Science, Technical Considerations and Clinical Aspects*. New York, NY: Springer New York, 2017.

Three Short - Three Long - Three Short

CQD *sécu*, from the French word *sécurité*, with the "D" added for "distress," was the earlier maritime code. "Mayday" was a term used in a voice message. In aviation, "pan-pan" was used, followed by a word describing an emergency.

All's Well

Photography by Emma Fairley of Chickadee Photography

Living in the Redline

J. Twenge et al. "Decreases in self-reported sleep duration in U.S. adolescents in 2009-2015 and association with new media screen time." *Sleep Medicine*. Vol. 37, November 2017, p. 47. doi: 10.1016/j.sleep.2017.08.013.

Healthy Hormones

Komer, Lawrence D., MD. "PTSD." In *New Hope for Concussions TBI & PTSD*. 1st ed. Toronto, ON: Peak Performance Institute, 2016.

    Adapted and used by permission of Peak Performance Institute.

Seasoned Travelers

Erik H. Erikson, Joan M. Erikson, The Life Cycle Completed: Extended Version (W. W. Norton, 1998), 111-112.

PTSD

Komer, Lawrence D., MD. "PTSD." In *New Hope for Concussions TBI & PTSD*. 1st ed. Toronto, ON: Peak Performance Institute, 2016.

    Adapted and used by permission of Peak Performance Institute.

Breathe: Your Spiritual Oasis

While I did the "resort course" back in the 1980s, I would recommend that anyone considering scuba diving take a full course offered by a certified instructor.

Make Your Prison Break

Cook, William S., Jr., and Grant D. Fairley. "Breaking the Chains." In *Your*

Third Act: A Guide to a Great Retirement. Chicago, IL: Silverwoods Publishing - a division of McK Consulting Inc, 2017.

This chapter is largely the same as our chapter "Breaking the Chains" in our earlier book, Your Third Act: A Guide to a Great Retirement. We believe these principles apply to all our relationships at every stage of life.

Resources

Personal and Professional Development

William S. Cook, Jr., M.D., is a board-certified outpatient psychiatrist who provides outpatient treatment in a confidential, private office setting in both Jackson, Mississippi, and Natchez, Mississippi. He may be contacted at www.williamscookjrmd.com or 4500 I-55 North, Suite 256, Jackson, MS 39211 or 601-366-3660.

Dr. Cook treats patients from ages 18 and upwards for a variety of psychiatric issues that include mood disorders, ADHD, relationship issues, and opioid dependence.

Strategic Seminars—Workshops and seminars for corporations and groups covering topics on business, leadership, motivation, relationships, team building, customer service, and more. There is a special focus on leadership and group development services for corporations. Seminars are offered in the US, Canada, and the Caribbean. www.strategic-seminars.com

Canadian Executive Coaching—Executive coaching for Canadian senior executives, managers, department heads, top salespeople, and leaders.

We serve a wide range of industry, government, and not-for-profit entities with one-on-one coaching to improve performance and provide personal support and reflection. Based on a whole-person model that recognizes our different skills, passions, and abilities, Canadian Executive Coaching will help you reach your full potential as a leader and as a person. This coaching service is now available worldwide. www.canadian-executive-coaching.com

Psycho-Geometrics® was created by Dr. Susan Dellinger, who used her skills as a communications specialist to design an incredibly intuitive yet accurate tool. It instantly identifies a person's communication style. The insight she had was to use the most common shapes of a circle, triangle, box, rectangle, and squiggly line. Once identified, she created very helpful descriptions that people usually find affirms their gut decision. Like a cool magic trick, you will want to know how she did it. This is one of the best ways to explore your communication styles, which are so important to effectiveness in business and in life relationships. If you have never heard Susan speak, read the book, or taken the Psycho-Geometrics® test, you are in for a great "aha!" moment. Take the online or print Psycho-Geometrics® test. Enter the promo code "Wheaton" and receive a discount. www.psychogeometrics.com

Blair Lamb, MD—Dr. Blair Lamb has practiced in the field of rehabilitative medicine for twenty-five years, using both non-interventional and interventional methods and modalities that facilitate the rehabilitation of most acute and chronic regional and global pain conditions. Dr. Lamb has multiple patents in spinal rehabilitation treatment, opiate side effect medication, opiate overuse medication, opiate withdrawal devices, trigger point dissolution medication, and shock wave

treatment. He has created advanced specific treatment protocols for complex conditions, such FMS (fibromyalgia syndrome), post-concussion syndrome, TMJ (temporomandibular joint syndrome), RSI (repetitive strain injury), RSD (reflex sympathetic dystrophy syndrome), dystonia (Parkinson's), migraine headache, and more. Dr. Lamb is a graduate of the University of Western Ontario Medical School. His practice is in Burlington, Ontario, Canada.
www.drlamb.com

Larry Komer, MD—His website offers information for women covering such topics as menopause, bio-identical hormone therapies, breast cancer, and more. For men, there is information about andropause, testosterone, fitness, and the various conditions affecting men. New understanding on traumatic brain injury is part of Dr. Komer's research as well.
www.drkomer.com
www.mastersmensclinic.com

A Wheaton Moment

Some people enjoy a very positive experience in their university lives. Others come to appreciate it more once they have moved on with their careers and personal lives. Those who enjoyed college life at the time and years later can also look back on it fondly have reason to be grateful.

For the authors in the late 1970s, Wheaton College, that small liberal arts Christian college west of Chicago, was such a place of positive memories. Founded in 1860, the academically rigorous college taught an integration of faith and learning that included attention to our development as whole persons. A Wheaton education included a call to serve others with whatever gifts, talents, and opportunities each was given.

Each class year consisted of only four hundred students from most of the fifty United States and many countries around the world. Experiencing community life at a residential college that included attention to our spiritual development gave us a valuable foundation for the years that would follow.

Led at the time by President Hudson Armerding, we were enriched by many wonderful professors who challenged and encouraged us. Like most alumni of any school, we look back on our years at the college as the best of times for us and for the institution.

We are grateful for the preparation Wheaton College gave us for our careers and our lives.

Silverwoods Publishing

Silverwoods Publishing - a division of McK Consulting Inc. shares books on leadership, retirement, compassion fatigue, finance, values, nostalgia, history, and life.

YOUR THIRD ACT

If life is a play with three acts in it, what will your third act be like?

Everyone approaching retirement have many questions.

What will it be like? What do I have to do to be ready? How will my life be different? Will these by my golden years or will this be a time of despair? If you are already retired, what can you do to make it a great time of life?

This book includes topics on: Family - Retirement – Purpose – Health – Friendships - Anti-aging – Meaning – Grief - Relationships – Brain Health - Legacy.

Discover the choices you can make to have a great retirement.

DISCOVER YOUR OASIS

Discover Your Oasis
Escape Compassion Fatigue

William S. Cook, Jr., M.D.
Grant D. Fairley

Psychiatrist William S. Cook, Jr., M.D. and executive coach Grant Fairley guide caregivers on how to find hope, refreshment, and satisfaction in their demanding careers. Compassion fatigue is an ever-present challenge for those who are committed to caring for and serving others. It is a resource for social workers, healthcare professionals, educators, ministers, first-responders, government, and leaders. It will also encourage those who care for a spouse or family member.

POSITIVE INFLUENCE

Leaders do not just play a role - they create a better future. Great leaders have discovered the value of influence, rather than control, as a leadership model. *Positive Influence - How to Lead Your World* is for those who are new to leadership and is a refresher for experienced leaders as well. This book is a professional development tool for leaders at any stage of their career.

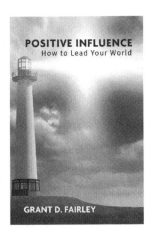

POSITIVE INFLUENCE
How to Lead Your World

GRANT D. FAIRLEY

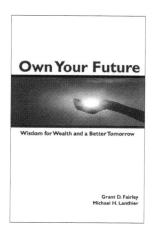

OWN YOUR FUTURE

This book is for everyone who wants to own their future. In a world where change is now normal, learn how to make career and financial decisions to build a better tomorrow for yourself and the ones you love. Whatever your age or stage in life, Fairley and Lanthier will show you how to have the courage to face your future with optimism and confidence.

UP TO THE COTTAGE

Up to the Cottage – Memories of Muskoka, which describes the joys and memories of simple cottages in the golden era of Muskoka. Grant D. Fairley recalls the heartwarming stories typical of life at cottages in the second half of the 20th Century. Whether you spent time in Muskoka, Haliburton, the Kawarthas, Door County in Wisconsin, the Adirondacks, or another place where cottages, cabins or camps were your home away from home, this book is for you.

THE FRIENDLY GIANT

Stroll back to your childhood with this book on the life and career of one of television's most memorable and endearing characters - The Friendly Giant. This show was part of the lives of generations of children, parents and grandparents who would wait to see the boot, watch the castle draw bridge lower and choose a chair by the fireplace weekday mornings on the NET (now PBS) Network in the U.S. and later CBC television in Canada. Memories of Friendly, Rusty, Jerome and the others will return as you read about this remarkable man and those who were a part of this great story. Grant D. Fairley was one of those children who grew up watching Friendly in Windsor, Ontario. Years later, he made the trip to Grafton, Ontario to meet Bob Homme and begin work on this authorized biography. Their many interviews during his retirement and the opportunity to meet others in Bob's story are here now for you to share.

THE MISADVENTURES OF HECTOR MACLEOD

This book was originally written in 1928. The tale is told with the care of a historian and a minister's love of story. Reverend Hugh Cowan transports his readers back to pioneer life in this wonderful and wild part of Canada at an important time in our history. Cowan grew up in the Manitoulin Island and La Cloche areas of Georgian Bay. He returned to it many times over his life with some of his family remaining on the island and in the region to this day.

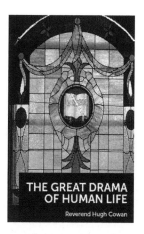

THE GREAT DRAMA OF HUMAN LIFE

In 1937, minister and historian Rev. Hugh Cowan reflects at the end of four decades of ministry on the some of the big ideas of the Christian faith. He recounts some of the changes he has observed in Christian thought in the first half of the 20th Century. In this book, Cowan explores the realities of life and death as experienced with his congregations. Many of the challenges he discusses are just as relevant today.

"This world's a stage, a poet once sung, and on it each man must act his part. Another poet has said, "Change and decay in all around I see."

Two poets, one sees in human life a great drama, and every member of the human family performing a part in that drama; the other sees in human life, change and death.

In the great drama of human life, the producer of the drama is God; the Lord Jesus supplies to the stage its light; while the Spirit of God is the One who trains and disciplines and practises the actors so that each may do their part wisely and well, even perfectly. The members of the human family, the actors on the stage, some do their part wisely and well, never perfectly; some do their part not so wisely and not so well; others do not do their part at all; while still others are out in rebellion to destroy the good influence and effect of the drama, if they can."

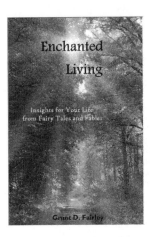

ENCHANTED LIVING

Grant's next book is based on the classic fairy tales and fables is Enchanted Living - Insights for Your Life from Fairy Tales & Fables. With the retelling of the traditional stories, Grant finds a new perspective, with an applications to life and business. These fairy tales have been a popular part of his seminar presentations over the past few years.

www.silverwoods-publishing.com
@silverwoodspub

About the Authors

William S. Cook, Jr., M.D.

Dr. William S. Cook, Jr., is a native of Jackson, Mississippi. His friendship with the coauthor started many years ago at Wheaton College where he majored in biology. He returned home to Jackson, Mississippi, to complete his medical school training at the University of Mississippi Medical School. He completed a flexible internship at Framingham Union Hospital in Framingham, Massachusetts, focusing on internal medicine. While pursuing an aspiration of being a dermatologist, Dr. Cook completed a year of pathology residency training at the Mallory Institute of Pathology at Boston City Hospital in Boston, Massachusetts. He then completed a National Institute of Health fellowship in dermatology at the University of California in San Francisco.

Still unclear of his final direction in medicine, Dr. Cook worked in emergency medicine in both California and Mississippi. He went back to school to complete his residency training in psychiatry at the University of Mississippi Medical Center in Jackson, Mississippi, where he served as chief resident during his senior year. He received the Jaquith Award for most outstanding resident his senior year.

Dr. Cook went on to complete a fellowship in Public Psychiatry at Columbia University in New York, along with a fellowship specializing in sexuality at Bellevue Hospital (NYU School of Medicine) in New York. He has been a psychiatrist for the last twenty-three years with a current private outpatient practice in Jackson, Mississippi, along with working part time in Natchez, Mississippi. He currently lives in Jackson, Mississippi, with his partner, Jay, and their French Bull Dog, Bonnie Blu. Dr. Cook has had the opportunity to travel worldwide to over sixty countries. He recently went to the Republic of the Congo and enjoyed seeing the lowland gorillas.

Bill would like to dedicate this book to his buddy, Chris Allen, who demonstrated compassion and encouragement during the writing of this book, as well as to the professional colleagues, family, and friends who have enriched his life over the years.

Follow Bill on Twitter @drwilliamscook

His Tumblr blog www.drbillcook.tumblr.com

Bill would welcome your comments on the book. You may contact him at cook@silverwoods-publishing.com.

Grant D. Fairley

Grant D. Fairley is a principal speaker with Strategic Seminars, a division of McK Consulting Inc. His seminars cover a wide range of topics, including leadership, finance, team building, sales training, relationships, personal development, motivation, creativity, and more.

He serves as an executive coach providing professional development, support, and perspectives to senior executives in business, government, sales, and other organizations.

Grant is a graduate of Wheaton College, Wheaton, Illinois.

Over the years, he has had a liberal arts life with a range of activities that include teaching, writing, and encouraging as common threads in the many roles.

His books include *Look Up—Way Up! The Friendly Giant: the biography of Robert Homme* and *Up to the Cottage: Memories of Muskoka*, a book about the love of old cottages and cottage life in the 1900s.

He coauthored with his friend and colleague, Michael H. Lanthier, *Own Your Future: Wisdom for Wealth and a Better Tomorrow.* This book introduces readers to the big ideas of personal investment and career planning. It is also helpful for perspectives on how to build wealth for the long term while making wise decisions along the way.

Grant's next book includes his unique perspectives on the classic fairy tales and fables, *Enchanted Living: Insights for Your Life from Fairy*

Tales & Fables. With the retelling of the traditional stories, Grant finds a new perspective with an application to life and business. These fairy tales have been a popular part of his seminar presentations over the past few years.

He is grateful for the many oasis moments that he shares with his wife and friend, Cari. He also finds joy from time with son Doug and Stephh, daughter Beth and Matt, daughter Emma, and son Scott. Charming Lucas in Liverpool is the first of the next generation of the Fairley family. Lucas keeps Doug and Stephh very busy, as any busy one-year-old is wont to do. With ancestors who came to Canada from Scotland and England in the 19th and 20th centuries, they would refer to Great Britain as, "The old country." Now, living in England, Doug can refer to Canada as, "The old country." Life has many unexpected twists and turns.

Grant would like to thank Dr. James and Rev. Beth Ernest, Stuart and Karen Fickett, Murray and Barb Knights, Joan Fulmer, Joan Komer, Mike and Michelle Lanthier, John Mateau, Maurice Muller, Peter Jarvis, Andras Rameshwar, Dave and Beth Saunders, Jim Sparks, and Jim Sparrow for their insights and kind encouragement.

Follow Grant on Twitter @grantfairley

Silverwoods
Publishing

Made in the USA
Columbia, SC
24 July 2018